THE WORLD'S MOST
EVIL MEN

THE WORLD'S MOST EVIL MEN

Text by Peter Salmon

An Hachette UK Company
www.hachette.co.uk

Summersdale Publishers
Part of Octopus Publishing Group Limited
Carmelite House
50 Victoria Embankment
LONDON
EC4Y 0DZ
UK

www.summersdale.com

The authorized representative in the EEA is Hachette Ireland, 8 Castlecourt Centre, Dublin 15, D15 XTP3, Ireland (email: info@hbgi.ie)

Printed and bound by Clays Ltd, Suffolk, NR35 1ED

ISBN: 978-1-83799-556-1

This FSC® label means that materials and other controlled sources used for the product have been responsibly sourced

MIX
Paper | Supporting responsible forestry
FSC® C104740

Substantial discounts on bulk quantities of Summersdale books are available to corporations, professional associations and other organizations. For details contact general enquiries: telephone: +44 (0) 1243 771107 or email: enquiries@summersdale.com.

THE WORLD'S MOST
EVIL MEN

Terrifying True Stories of the Most
Notorious Men Throughout History

JAMIE KING

summersdale

CONTENTS

SERIAL KILLERS AND PSYCHOPATHS . . . 112

CULT LEADERS AND MANIPULATORS . . . 190

INTRODUCTION

Evil. There are those who say it doesn't exist. There are only evil acts, not evil men.

They should read this book. It will change their minds.

Here you will find men whose commitment to doing wrong dominated their lives. Sometimes they did it with a gun, sometimes with a bomb, sometimes with a knife. There are also those who did it with a fountain pen. A great many of them did it with a smile – there is nothing which drives a man to the extremes of evil more surely than to take pleasure in it. Anyone can become a victim of a man who desires to hurt them, and no rational argument will stop them in their tracks.

Some of the names will be familiar to you – Adolf Hitler, Jeffrey Dahmer, Jack the Ripper, Charles Manson, Saddam Hussein. These are men whose evil goes before them; they are names which can make us sick with fear at just the mention.

But evil doesn't always proclaim itself to the world; sometimes it exists in the shadows. Sometimes it can be a man like Adolf Eichmann, a quiet nonentity who oversaw the deportation of Jews to the gas chamber and who was described as showing the "banality of evil". Sometimes it can exist in places most of us have never considered, like a small village in rural China, where Yang Xinhai took the lives of 67 people and raped 23 women.

Whether a dictator or tyrant, a serial killer, psychopath or drug dealer, what joins these men in their unholy congress is the fact that they made the lives of those around them a misery and the world a worse place. Sometimes you can't help but feel that the luckiest of their victims merely died – a quick death when confronted by these monsters being the better option than the pain and degradation they spread. But a grave is still a grave, and there are millions of them because of the men gathered here.

The names of some of these men live on in infamy, while some are rarely remembered – but no problem, because when one evil man dies, there is always another to take his place. Like weeds in the garden of humanity, if you tear one out, another will grow in its place – and it will often be stronger than the one you removed. As the philosopher Pascal put it, "Evil is easy, and has infinite forms."

So join us on a journey to the darkest recesses of the human heart, where cult leaders and mass murderers jostle with tyrants and serial killers, and where criminal masterminds and those who plan for world domination live alongside torturers and sadists. This is a world where troubled hearts and troubled minds drive men to places where no good man would go, and where the game of justice is stacked against those who desire the triumph of truth and decency. And if it can dwell in any heart, then it can dwell in every heart.

As a wise man once said, "The only thing necessary for the triumph of evil is for good men to do nothing." Which side are you on?

ANCIENT MALEVOLENCE

It is said that evil entered the world when Eve bit the apple in the Garden of Eden. Well, that is one possibility. But it seems that the human heart has known evil since the moment it started beating, and that evil has dwelt most successfully in the hearts of men.

In this chapter we will meet some individuals who lived their lives not for the glory of mankind, but for its disgrace. From the Roman emperor Caligula, who even his friends described as cruel, sadistic and sexually perverted, to the Romanian ruler Vlad the Impaler, whose actions were so despicable that he would be the inspiration for Dracula, these are men whose treachery still revolts down through the centuries.

But a man need not rule a country to spread evil in his wake – Tomás de Torquemada and Godfrey of Bouillon did it while carrying a Bible, Dhu Shanatir did it with tempting offers of food. One need only have a black spot in one's heart. In the case of some of these men, the whole heart seems to have been black. No light escapes from it, and no victim escapes from them.

And no matter how far back in the past they are, don't forget, today will be the ancient past one day, and who knows which men will be spoken of with terror in the future, who will be our Caligulas and Draculas? What form will they take, and what new entries will they make in the book of evil?

CALIGULA

You don't need to read up on the lives of many Roman emperors to know that evil was not an abstract concept to many of them. From Elagabalus, whose sexual and religious perversions were so extreme that the historian Gibbon wrote, "Elagabalus had nothing at all to make up for his vices, which are of such a kind that it is too disgusting even to allude to them;" to Tiberius, who spent most of his reign brutally murdering his enemies and then, having run out of them, brutally murdering his friends. Being Roman emperor is no job for the faint- or pure-hearted.

So to take the laurel as the most evil Roman emperor is no mean feat, and there are really only two men in the running: Nero and his uncle Caligula. If Caligula just shades it, it's because he got in first with many of the evil vices his nephew would later glory in.

Gaius Caesar Augustus Germanicus, better known by his nickname Caligula, was born in 12 CE, the son of a general. His nickname means "little boot", in reference to the military clothes his father dressed him in. Adopted by Tiberius – who recognized the boy was as evil as himself and declared he was "nursing a viper in Rome's bosom" – Caligula was 24 when he ascended to the throne on the death of Tiberius in 37 CE. By the age of 28, he was dead, assassinated by the notoriously unsentimental Praetorian Guard, for whom Caligula's actions were too hard to stomach.

Most of Caligula's reign was spent glorifying himself – using the money of the state to build vast palaces for himself and giant statues in his own honour. He declared himself a living God and ordered the population to worship him as ardently as they worshipped their other gods. In fact, more ardently, for by his reckoning he was the greatest of these deities.

He expanded his powers until they became absolute – so much so that he was delighted to appoint his own horse as consul and leader of the Senate. According to his biographer Suetonius, Caligula's favourite phrase was, "Remember that I have the right to do anything to anybody."

This included the personal humiliation of those around him – he would force senators to run in front of his chariot, with those who stumbled or fell being crushed beneath it. All women were to be available to him – he had the wives of allies brought to his bed and is rumoured to have slept with his own sisters. After sleeping with a man's wife, he would bring the husband before him and humiliate him with details of his wife's sexual performance.

Such was Caligula's love of money that he would have piles of it strewn around his palace, just so he could roll around in it. He was known to take pearls from women's necks, dissolve them and drink them from goblets of wine, just because he could. He confiscated many of the estates of the wealthy, adding the money to his own coffers.

Those who met Caligula always called him extremely ugly and goat-like – in fact, he made it an offence punishable by death to mention a goat in his presence. In fact, the list of capital offences grew and grew under his reign – no one could be sure what behaviour might next be punishable by death. Eventually these offences were not dictated by law, but by his own whims. No one was safe from the executioner's blade.

And in the end, nor was Caligula. A group of senators and the Praetorian Guard, disgusted by the shame that Caligula had brought to the office of emperor and the shame he had brought to the entire Roman empire, decided it was time to end his reign by a method as bloody as he had used to end the lives of so many. Praetorian tribunes Cassius Chaerea and Cornelius Sabinus, as well as a number of centurions, accosted Caligula just outside one of his palaces as he gave a speech.

He was stabbed over and over by the conspirators, as were his wife and daughter – the guards wanted to wipe the line of Caligula from Roman history (although his nephew Nero, also evil and who also gets an entry in this book, would also become emperor). Few, if any, mourned Caligula's death. As the historian Cassius Dio wrote a century later, Caligula "learned by actual experience that he was not a god".

GENGHIS KHAN

He wasn't born Genghis Khan – his original name, given to him in 1155, was Temüjin, which means "blacksmith". He was the son of a tribal Mongolian chieftain named Yesugei, and according to legend, his birth was auspicious because he came into the world holding a clot of blood in his hand.

But when Temüjin was nine, Yesugei was poisoned, and Temüjin's family was cast out by their tribe and fell into extreme poverty. It seemed the young boy was to live a life of poor obscurity, however auspicious his birth.

And yet by the time Genghis Khan died, he was the ruler of the largest empire the world had ever seen, stretching 23 million kilometres, encompassing Japan and Eastern Europe in the east, the Indian subcontinent and Iran in the south, and spreading west across what we now call the Middle East, into the Carpathian Mountains, which run across southern Europe. The empire's population of 110 million meant one in four people on Earth was ruled by Khan.

He was known for demanding and giving complete loyalty to his friends, and for his bloodthirsty dealings with his enemies. You don't get to conquer most of the world by being nice to people.

Khan's evil streak revealed itself when he was 14. He had an older half-brother, Behter, to whom the meagre family rations and property went first. Temüjin killed him, thus securing his place as the head of the family. It was the first of many rises from his lowly station.

Khan was known for his charisma and soon used this to secure the friendship of two local chieftains named Jamukha and Toghrul. When he fell out with Jamukha in 1187, they went to war. Temüjin lost and for the next nine years was a subject of the Jin dynasty. He used the time to plot his path to power. First, he defeated Toghrul, then he launched an attack on Jamukha. Defeating his army, Temüjin killed Jamukha in front of the vanquished soldiers with his own hands, reciting as he did what became his first law of engagement – "Never betray your Khan."

His rapidly expanding army began to amass a series of victories that astonished the world and continue to astonish us now. Army after army fell to him, and he was ruthless in his methods. No leader was ever allowed to survive, so none could stab him in the back. He also made sure that any other members of the leader's clan were exterminated.

The enemy army was also routed – he was not one who took prisoners of war; only death awaited the defeated. He even went into conquered villages and eliminated any possible future heroes – it is said he would kill any man taller than the height of a cart axle.

By 1206, he was the leader of the entire Eurasian Steppe, encompassing everywhere from Hungary to Ukraine and southern Russia, from Kazakhstan to South Asia. He adopted the name Genghis Khan. Khan means ruler, but there are debates around the meaning of Genghis. The most likely option is that it derives from the word for "ocean", and Genghis Khan truly was the ruler of the world up to and including the oceans around Europe and Asia.

His ruthlessness was legendary – he was known never to leave a score unsettled. For instance, in 1219, when the Shah of the Khwarezmian Empire in Persia (now Iran) broke a trade treaty with the Mongols, Khan's response was swift and brutal. His army went in and killed everyone. Millions were left dead, and a 200-year-old empire simply disappeared.

It was not the only such act – the population of China fell by tens of millions during his reign, and conservative estimates believe around 40 million people were killed by his armies. This means Genghis Khan killed around 11 per cent of the world's population, over one in ten people.

His own death was anticlimactic – it is said that he died in 1229 from injuries sustained when he fell from his horse. No one knows where he was buried – his funeral procession was ordered to slaughter anyone they encountered along the trail; it is understood that those on the procession who knew the exact location were also killed to keep the knowledge secret.

His death was not the end of the Mongol Empire, which would continue to expand under a series of his descendants, perhaps the most famous of whom was Kublai Khan (ruled 1271–1294). On Kublai's death, the empire descended into civil war, then gradually petered out.

But the Mongol Empire under Genghis Khan has never been exceeded in terms of sheer size, and its first ruler remains one of the most ruthless and pitiless men ever to walk the earth.

VLAD THE IMPALER

The clue is in the nickname. If you are known by your favourite method of killing your enemies, it is a fair bet you are pretty evil. And the man who was the Ruler of Wallachia (in Romania) between 1456 and 1462, and again between 1475 and 1477, was evil enough that he was the inspiration for one of the most terrifying characters of all time, Dracula.

In fact, it was his father who was first given the name "Dracul", which means "Dragon" – "Dracul-a" means "Son of the Dragon".

Vlad senior seems to have been a wise and tolerant leader – he fought wars, but there are few reports of atrocities beyond those that come with any war. Vlad junior was the second of four sons, and he and his younger brother Radu spent much of their early life held by the Turks of the Ottoman Empire under Mehmed II in return for their father's obedience.

And there he might have stayed, except that in 1447, his father and older brother were killed by the Wallachian boyars (nobles). Leaving his other brother Radu behind, Vlad would spend the next eight years fighting to reclaim the throne – and his methods would go down in history as an example of pure evil.

What is impaling? The victim is shackled, and then a metal or wooden pole is forced through their body vertically, through the rectum or vagina, emerging through the neck, shoulders or mouth. This was done as slowly as possible. Vlad preferred a rounded pole rather than a sharp one – that way no internal organs would be pierced, so the victim would remain alive the entire time.

Ideally, the victim would then be raised vertically and placed on public display so that their death torment could be watched. It generally took hours for them to die, but some lasted several days, all of it spent in agony. This was the fate of any boyar Vlad could lay his hands on.

But it was not just the nobles who Vlad killed, and he was happy to use other methods. As he boasted in a letter to an ally about one campaign against his former Ottoman captors, "I have killed peasants, men and women, old and young… We killed 23,884 Turks, without counting those whom we burned in homes or the Turks whose heads were cut by our soldiers."

By 1456, he had reclaimed the throne, but there was no rest for his enemies. He continued his wholesale slaughter in order to consolidate his position and made sure any potential threats were neutralized. For instance, when he came into conflict with the Transylvanian Saxons in 1460, Vlad plundered the Saxon villages, taking the captured people back to Wallachia, where he had them impaled.

By now his reputation was spreading throughout Europe. Legend had it that he liked to dine in the middle of a "forest" of defeated enemies, devouring his meal as they writhed on poles around him. It was even claimed that he dipped his bread in their blood before eating it.

When the Ottoman army attempted to invade the Romanian villagers of Târgoviște, Vlad's forces repelled them and then impaled some 20,000 villagers and captured soldiers who were placed in a circle around the village. Mehmed II was so disgusted by the scale of Vlad's carnage and the thousands of decaying bodies being picked apart by crows that he retreated forever.

Vlad's younger brother Radu had by now risen through the Ottomans' ranks and became one of Mehmed II's closest confidantes. Known as Radu the Handsome, he led armies against his older brother, and although Vlad won each encounter, more and more Wallachians, horrified by their leader's actions, joined the Ottoman army. Weakened, in 1462, Vlad sought help from Matthias Corvinus, King of Hungary. The last thing Corvinus wanted was to fight the Ottomans. Instead, he imprisoned Vlad, and Radu was installed on the throne.

For the next 13 years, Vlad the Impaler was held captive in Visegrád in Hungary. On his release in 1475, he managed to reclaim the throne, but his reign was to be a short one; he was killed in battle in 1477.

After his death, his legend continued to grow, both as a hero of the defence of Wallachia from the Ottomans and as a great villain whose bloodthirsty ways were almost unrivalled in human history. Throughout Europe, parents would scare their children with stories of Vlad the Impaler, who consumed the blood of his victims.

No one quite knows how a then virtually unknown Irishman named Bram Stoker first heard about Vlad, but sometime in the 1890s, he began writing a novel about a Transylvanian nobleman, Count Dracula, who drank blood in order to survive. The book was an immediate hit, and it remains one of the most famous novels of all time, continuing to inspire sequels in both print and film.

Perhaps terrible Vlad has had his final revenge on Radu the Handsome, who no one has ever been inspired to write a novel about?

DHU SHANATIR

His name means "The Man with Earrings". His province, the Himyarite Kingdom – modern-day Yemen – which he ruled from 490 to 517 CE. His perversion – young boys.

Little is known about him, although we do know he was not next in line for the throne when the previous king died. There was a huge battle for the kingship, and Dhu Shanatir was merciless in achieving his goal. Reports from the time have nothing good to say of him, describing him as "cruel and oppressive". The princes he defeated in the battle for the throne were tortured and killed. His subjects hated him, but they feared him too, and he was able to govern without any rebellion being organized. For 27 years he rode roughshod over the Himyarites.

In truth, his kingdom was not large, being made up of many separate tribes, and his name may well have been lost to history in the same way as most of the Himyarite rulers, were it not for the particular strain of evil which infected him. It is down to this that his name continues to be spoken.

Dhu Shanatir loved young boys, and he loved to kidnap them and use them for his sexual pleasure. We don't know the numbers involved, but we do know it ran to the hundreds. We also know that when he had taken his pleasure, he was not one to keep his victim. Instead, he would throw them from the highest window of his stone palace. The sound of a naked body hitting the ground would alert his guard that another boy was required.

The only other fact that has come down to us from history is the way that Dhu Shanatir died. A young man called Zur'ah went to visit the king and had a dagger hidden in his shoe. He knew the king's tastes and dressed in a way to tempt the monarch. When the king pounced, Zur'ah stabbed him to death – legend has it that he did so from behind, in the position where the king had committed his most terrible crimes.

So happy were the Himyarites that they declared Zur'ah king. He only reigned for eight years, most of which he spent persecuting Christians, until a Christian army was raised against him, and he killed himself by riding his horse into the Red Sea.

Zur'ah's death marked the end of the Himyarite kingdom.

MARQUIS
DE SADE

If a man can be convicted as evil for what goes on in his head as much as what he does in his life, then surely the Marquis de Sade deserves to be listed in any catalogue of infamy. The books he wrote, describing erotic tortures and murders, were so extreme as to see him imprisoned, and he has given his name to the pursuit of pleasure by causing pain – "sadism".

Born into the nobility in Paris in 1740, his best-known pornographic works, *The 120 Days of Sodom*, *Justine*, *Juliette* and *Philosophy in the Bedroom*, include graphic descriptions of sex acts, rape, torture, murder and child abuse. They also include discussions of politics, philosophy and religion, and for some he is as much to be remembered for this as his depravities.

This depravity surfaced early, and as a child he was known for his violent rages. In the autumn of 1750, ten-year-old Sade was sent to the Jesuit college Louis-le-Grand in Paris, and some have speculated that the regular canings, which were part of the school's methods of punishment, may have given him a taste for the lash. He may have also been sodomized by older students, a not uncommon occurrence at the time.

He joined the army. He married. He had three children. But all the while his sexual desires became more and more perverse. He would regularly pay prostitutes to come to his house, where he would subject them to violent sexual abuse. One, Jeanne Testard, told police that Sade had asked her whether she believed in God. When she said that she did, Sade said there was no God and shouted obscenities concerning Jesus and the Virgin Mary. Then he masturbated with a chalice and crucifix while shouting blasphemies and asked her to engage in sodomy, then illegal. He was sent to prison for blasphemy.

Sade would spend the next few years in and out of jail. In 1768, he kidnapped 36-year-old Rose Keller, tied her to a bed, whipped her, cut her and dripped hot wax in the wounds. He locked her in an upstairs room, but she managed to escape and alert the authorities. Jailed again and released again, he committed his next punishable offence in 1772, when he and his manservant Latour took part in an orgy with four prostitutes, which entailed flagellation and sodomy. Sade also fed the prostitutes food containing the aphrodisiac Spanish Fly in such large doses they almost died.

This time he was sentenced to death for sodomy and poisoning, but he had already gone into hiding in Italy. When the prostitutes withdrew their complaints, his sentence was commuted to imprisonment, and he gave himself up. He spent the next year in prison in Sardinia, before escaping and returning to France.

But Sade's lusts were unsated. In 1774, he engaged in a series of sadomasochistic orgies with servants newly employed at his property, most of whom were around 15 years old. Fleeing again to Italy, he spent a year in hiding – his first book was a travel guide to Italy! – then returned to France for more debauchery and more arrests. On 26 August 1778, he was arrested again and placed in a fortress in Vincennes in eastern Paris for what was supposed to be a long stretch.

In prison, he began writing in earnest – as well as the travel book, he produced *The 120 Days of Sodom*, in which his sexual peccadilloes appeared in fictional form. It is the story of four wealthy libertine Frenchmen who spend four months seeking the ultimate sexual gratification through orgies with 12 accomplices, 20 designated victims and ten servants. All the victims, locked in a castle with their tormentors, undergo brutal sexual abuse and torture, including coprophilia, necrophilia, bestiality, incest, rape and child sexual abuse. No book more shocking has ever been released – even 200 years later, Pier Paolo Pasolini's movie *Salo*, based on the book, was banned in most countries.

Released in 1790 by the new government after the French Revolution, the 55-year-old Sade concentrated on his work as a writer and became involved in politics. Divorcing his wife, he began a relationship with Marie-Constance Quesnet, a 33-year-old actress, and the two would stay together until his death.

But his freedom only lasted just over a decade. Arrested again in 1801 during a crackdown on public morality, he was imprisoned without trial, as the government thought a trial would just increase his notoriety. In prison, he returned to some of his former ways, attempting to seduce fellow inmates, and he was soon transferred to an asylum. Marie-Constance, pretending to be his illegitimate daughter, was allowed to live with him there.

Sade continued to write, including a ten-volume novel, and put on plays at a theatre built in the asylum. But his health was deteriorating, and in 1814, he died of gangrene at the grand age of 74.

The crimes he wrote of were greater than the crimes he committed, but there seems little doubt he would have carried out his fictional crimes in real life if there were no consequences. For some, he is the great libertine, imagining a world where all could be free to pursue those desires. But it seems a world few of us would want to live in.

JUDAS

How wicked do you have to be for your name to be a byword for evil? Many of the men in this book have carried out atrocious acts, killed and maimed countless victims, dragged huge numbers of people into battle and followed sadistic impulses, unconstrained by nature or society. But one man carries the taint of evil for one particular act – a kiss.

We know little about Judas Iscariot. His forename was a common one in the first century CE – in fact, we are only told his second name to distinguish him from Judas Thaddeus. Both were apostles, those 12 men chosen by Jesus to be his closest followers.

According to the Gospel of John, Judas Iscariot was the treasurer of the group, and virtually the only reference to him apart from his final act of betrayal is that he grew angry when an expensive jar of oil used to anoint Jesus was broken. Other than that, we know nothing – until the night of the Last Supper.

As we are very familiar with from the famous painting by Leonardo da Vinci, Jesus and the 12 apostles gathered for supper on the night before Passover. There Jesus broke bread, which he said was his body, and offered around wine, which he said was his blood. These acts would become the institution of the Mass in Christian ritual.

Jesus also made a prediction that shocked the apostles – one of those seated there would betray him before the night was out. After the supper, Jesus took the apostles to the Garden of Gethsemane to pray. Judas slipped away and came back with the soldiers of the High Priest Caiaphas.

Confronted with Jesus and the 11 others, the soldiers needed to know which was the one who had proclaimed himself the Messiah. Judas identified Jesus by kissing him on the cheek. Jesus was arrested, turned over to the local governor Pontius Pilate, and, as we know, put to death.

According to the Gospel of Matthew, Judas exchanged the life of Jesus for "30 pieces of silver" – an act of avarice in stark contrast to the self-sacrifice of Jesus. To this day the phrase "30 pieces of silver" remains an insult, while a Judas Kiss remains the ultimate form of betrayal.

Given that Judas believed Jesus was either the Son of God, or at least a prophet and saviour, this was an act of terrible horror. It was not just one man who Judas betrayed, but in one sense, the whole world. It doesn't get much more evil than that.

There are differing versions of what happened to Judas next. According to the Gospel of Matthew, Judas was overcome with remorse and attempted to return the money, but the priests refused to take it. He threw it back at them and then went and hung himself. The priests used the money to buy a field now called Akeldama, the Field of Blood, which is still part of Jerusalem.

In another story, from the fourth century CE, Judas went home to his wife, who was cooking a chicken, and told her he was going to kill himself. She said that Jesus was as likely to rise from the dead as the chicken – and the chicken promptly came back to life. Judas hung himself immediately.

There are those, however, who dispute the idea that Judas was evil – a Gospel of Judas, composed in 200 CE and rediscovered in the 1970s, says that Jesus told Judas to betray him, in order to carry out God's plan for Jesus to save all souls by being crucified, and then return three days later. This would in fact make Judas the closest confidante of Jesus and would be an act of sacrifice beyond all measure – to allow his own name to go down in infamy to carry out the Lord's plan.

But few agree with this idea, and if we want the most common judgement on Judas, we need look no further than that great poem by Dante, the fourteenth-century epic, *The Inferno*. Moving slowly down the "seven circles of hell", the poet finally reaches the last circle, named Judecca – after Judas himself – and there, frozen in ice, placed head-first inside three-headed Lucifer's central mouth, with his back skinned by the devil's claw, is the man Dante calls the greatest sinner of all time – Judas Iscariot.

QIN SHI HUANG

He is best known outside of China for the terracotta army guarding his mausoleum, which was discovered by accident in 1974. These 2,000 figures, each unique, stand guard at his burial place and are joined by terracotta acrobats, musicians and water birds. It is believed there are over 6,000 stone statues still to be unearthed – a huge militia but fitting for the man who was the first of 559 emperors of China, Qin Shi Huang.

But if his new fame rests on this astonishing archaeological find, it was as a tyrant that he was famous in earlier times. The sort of influence that he wielded is not done so gently. China remains one of the largest countries in the world, and it was Qin Shi Huang who bound it together by force of will and a willingness to ignore his conscience.

He was born as Ying Zheng in 259 BCE, at a time known in China as the Warring States period, which had begun in 475 BCE and would continue until his final victory. Seven states vied for dominance in China, and his father was king of one of them, the Qin. On his father's death, 13-year-old Ying Zheng assumed the throne of Qin.

He was to prove a brilliant and ruthless ruler, and his ruthlessness was on display soon after he took the crown. Unbeknown to him, the man acting as his regent, Lü Buwei, was having an affair with his mother. Fearful he would be found out, Lü Buwei raised an army of hundreds and organized a coup against the boy king.

Ying Zheng's reaction was swift and pitiless. He routed the army, killing all of them. The army's leader fled the battlefield, and the king placed a ransom on him: 1 million copper coins if the leader was taken alive or half a million if dead. He was taken alive. The boy king watched as the leader was torn apart by five horses, and then commanded that his entire family be killed, to the third degree of relation. He locked up his own mother, and Lü Buwei killed himself. Ying Zheng understood that mercy is a form of weakness.

Over the next 25 years, Ying Zheng pursued a policy of carnage. Men, women and children were put to the sword, villages razed, alliances made then broken, opposition armies remorselessly destroyed. Gradually he began to unify China.

Twice he survived assassination attempts. The first time, a dagger was drawn on him by a man pretending to be a diplomat. It was the king himself who drew his sword and killed the attacker, as none of his bodyguards were allowed to carry swords in case they themselves tried to kill the king.

The second time, a famous lute player, Gao Jianli, was summoned to play for the king. He was recognized before the concert as a friend of the first assassin. But Ying Zheng still wished to hear the music, so he hit on a simple solution – he had the musician's eyes put out. He then kept Gao Jianli on as a court musician. The blind man performed for Ying Zheng regularly, until he attempted to strike the king with a lute weighed down with lead. Then he was executed in front of the court.

By 221 BCE, Ying Zheng had defeated all six other warring states, and all of China was his. He had himself crowned as emperor and took the name Qin Shi Huang, meaning first emperor.

He set about reforming China in his own image, bringing in many of the laws that would exist until the twentieth century. His system of government would endure until 1911. He also began the construction of one of the most astonishing architectural feats of humankind, the Great Wall of China, to defend the northern frontier of his new empire.

Having seen and caused so much death, Qin Shi Huang became obsessed with his own. He studied alchemy and tried hard to find the elixir of life. He sought magicians who claimed to know how to forestall death and was known to bury them alive to test their claims. He attempted to burn all the books in the empire that were not alchemical or dealt with medicine.

His search for immortality was unsuccessful. In July or August 210 BCE, he died. But what no one knew until 29 March 1974, when a farmer found fragments of pottery while digging a well, was that he had been buried with a retinue fit for an emperor. It has been estimated it would have needed a team of 700,000 forced labour conscripts to construct the mausoleum, many of whom no doubt died – the final victims of one of the most ruthless men who ever lived.

TORQUEMADA

They were given a simple but ill-defined task – to "uphold Catholic religious orthodoxy" in what had just become the Kingdom of Spain. With Castile and Aragon being joined together, a diverse population had been created, which included Jews and Muslims. This was seen as a threat to the new Catholic monarchs of Spain, Queen Isabella I of Castile and King Ferdinand II of Aragon. Their marriage in 1469 had brought the kingdom together. And now the pair wanted to purge it.

But who would take charge of cleansing Spain of heretics? Queen Isabella had an answer. As a young girl she had met a prior at the monastery of Segovia who had become her regular confessor and personal advisor – it was he who had suggested her marriage to Ferdinand. His name was Tomás de Torquemada, and over the course of 15 years he would perform acts of such barbarism that his name has become synonymous with cruelty, religious intolerance and fanaticism.

From an early age, Torquemada had been a zealous Catholic, fighting against perceived threats to the church. Born in 1420, at an early age he entered the local monastery, San Pablo Dominican, before being promoted to prior, which was where he met Princess Isabella. Staying close to the princess, and later to her husband the king, he was perfectly positioned in 1478, when the pope decreed a crackdown on religious heresy, to lead what was officially known as the Holy Office for the Propagation of the Faith, but which was soon known by a name which still induces terror – The Spanish Inquisition.

As Grand Inquisitor, Torquemada announced 28 articles for the guidance of inquisitors, covering such crimes as heresy, apostasy, sorcery, sodomy, polygamy, blasphemy and usury. The articles gave the inquisitors full power to torture confessions out of the suspects, and Torquemada led by example in the severity and depravity of these measures.

The tortures began on arrest and continued throughout the interrogation. Methods included the rack, where the suspects had their body pulled to its limits; the pulley, in which the suspects had their hands tied behind their backs, were hoisted off the ground by their wrists by a pulley attached to a beam and then dropped repeatedly, dislocating the shoulders and leaving the victims hanging in a position where breathing was difficult; and the "water cure", where suspects were forced to drink gallons of water until they were near death.

Every suspect was presumed guilty; they were not there to argue their innocence but to confess. After confession, the horrors didn't stop – many were put to death by *auto-da-fé*, which literally translates to "act of faith" but in practical terms meant being garrotted and then burned alive.

Various estimates have been given for the number of deaths Torquemada supervised, but a figure of 2,000 seems likely. But killing heretics was not his only pleasure. He also oversaw the expulsion of approximately 40,000 Jews in 1492 and the forced conversion of another 50,000, all of whom would have been threatened with torture or death; many of these people had to endure the former until they renounced their Jewish faith.

So extreme was Torquemada that even the Pope who had ordered the Inquisition felt compelled to step in. Three times Torquemada was summoned to Rome and told to stop; three times he returned to Spain and carried on his work.

Eventually even the king and queen turned against him, not only because of the cruelty but also because of the vast sums of money he was spending tracking down suspects and inventing new and more terrible ways to torture and kill them. The royals worked with the Pope to strip Torquemada of his power, and in 1494, he was retired to the monastery of St Thomas Aquinas in Ávila, where he lived the simple life of a monk.

The Spanish Inquisition would continue in various forms until 1834, but never with the cruelty it had under Torquemada. He died as a man content with his achievements, believing in the holiness of his mission.

Others disagreed. In 1832, his bones were dug up and burned – the final victim of *auto-da-fé* in the Spanish Inquisition.

ANDRONIKOS I KOMNENOS

His reign was mercifully short, a mere two years, but in that time Andronikos I Komnenos really got a lot of evil done. As Emperor of Byzantine from 1183 to 1185, he instituted a reign of terror so extreme that eventually he was torn to pieces in the street by his own citizens. If all we knew about him was his nickname – "Misophaes", meaning "Hater of Sunlight", given to him for the number of his enemies he had blinded – that would be enough. Unfortunately for our faith in humanity, we know a whole lot more.

Born into the Golden Age of Byzantium – an age he would go a long way to ending – in 1118, he was known from his youth as handsome and courageous, excelling as a soldier when he began his military service. He was also known for his lusts – his dedication to the army was only matched by his dedication to pleasure.

In 1142, he held a position at the court of his cousin, Emperor Manuel I Komnenos, and began an affair with his own niece, Eudoxia. Soon after, he was almost killed by Eudoxia's brothers.

The reason has been lost, but based on later behaviour, we can hazard a guess – his intentions may not have been honourable.

The emperor, however, was a huge admirer of the military skill of Andronikos, who won a number of decisive victories against their enemy Hungary. But playing second fiddle was not Andronikos' style. In 1153, the emperor discovered that his power-hungry cousin was conspiring against him and imprisoned him. But when Hungary invaded, the emperor pardoned Andronikos, who then led the army to another glorious victory.

Andronikos returned to court, where he immediately seduced another of his own nieces, Theodora, with whom he had children, and then began again to conspire against the emperor. Removed from the court, he spent the next two decades as both a sword for hire around Europe and the Middle East, and a serial seducer, being chased out of country after country after bedding young women of high rank, even as he approached the age of 60.

In 1180, he returned to Byzantium, prostrating himself before the emperor in chains. Pardoned again, he was sent into exile on the Black Sea coast. It seemed Andronikos would spend his last years in gentle retirement.

However, later the same year, Emperor Manuel died at the age of 62. The heir to the throne was the emperor's son, ten-year-old Alexios II, who was under the guardianship of his mother, Maria of Antioch. Maria was a Catholic, and the Orthodox population of Byzantium soon turned against her. Sensing his chance, Andronikos raised an army and marched on the capital, Constantinople. He met no resistance. Alexios II and Maria were arrested, and Andronikos was made co-emperor with Alexios.

He inherited a population angered by Manuel's pro-Western leanings. They soon rose up and carried out what became known as the Massacre of the Latins. Some 60,000 Catholics were killed in less than a month.

Andronikos did not order the massacre, but nor did he step in. What he did do was have Empress Maria executed, either by being beheaded or by being tied in a sack and drowned. Soon after, Alexios was strangled to death, after being made to sign his own death warrant, and Andronikos became the sole emperor of Byzantium. No one knew it then, but he was to be the last emperor of the 120-year-old Komnenos dynasty. He would destroy it in two years.

His first act was one of depravity – the 65-year-old married the widow of Alexios, 12-year-old Agnes of France. More depravity soon followed – he did not just attempt to limit the power of the nobility – his potential enemies – he slaughtered them, and he put out the eyes of any court official or general he suspected of disloyalty.

No one was safe. Not satisfied with killing nobles, he started killing the general population, attacking villages and impaling citizens around the walls as a warning to all who would oppose him.

So obsessed was he with the enemies within that he forgot the enemies without, and Hungary and Serbia picked off a number of the frontiers of his empire. When 80,000 Sicilians invaded in 1185, taking the major Byzantine city of Thessaloniki, his subjects looked to Andronikos to defend them. But he was too busy with a plan to kill all remaining nobles.

The people turned to a general, Isaac Angelos, and declared him emperor. Andronikos fled but was captured and brought before the new emperor. Isaac decided it was for the people to administer justice. Andronikos, who had marched into Constantinople in triumph two years earlier, had his teeth and hair pulled out, boiling water poured on his face and his right arm cut off, before being paraded around the streets strapped to a camel. He was then beaten again – all by the very mob who had cheered his arrival.

His torment ended three days later, when he was tied upside down to two pillars by his ankles and torn limb from limb by the crowd, his bones fed to the dogs. There were, no doubt, a number of newly blind men there, wishing they could see the last moments of Andronikos I Komnenos, Emperor of Byzantium.

KING JOHN

It is the most common name in English, yet no king since 1216 has decided to call themselves John, as a direct result of one man who desecrated the name forever. King John is best known as a pantomime villain, as opposed to the noble Robin Hood, who steals from the rich and gives to the poor. In popular culture, it is King John who is constantly foiled by Robin and ends up looking a fool. It is a caricature of the real John but firmly based on truth.

Was he evil? He was certainly, according to all who knew him, unpleasant. He was also incompetent – he managed during his reign to lose most of the French lands won in several bloody battles by Britain, almost without a whimper. He also caused a revolt among the barons and was so weak that he was forced to sign the Magna Carta, which, in one fell swoop, took away most of the powers of the monarch. And he liked starving people to punish them.

Perhaps if he had not been king, he would have been free to be unpleasant and incompetent on a small, anonymous scale. But as king, this unpleasantness and incompetence gave weight to his foolish and petty acts – they in time became evil ones.

Born in 1166, the youngest of five sons of King Henry II of England and Duchess Eleanor of Aquitaine, he was commonly known as John Lackland – John without land – and was expected to inherit nothing, least of all the crown. But when three of his brothers, Henry, Richard and the illegitimate eldest Geoffrey, joined Eleanor in rebelling against the king and were defeated, he shot up the list of heirs to second place. His brother Richard the Lionheart succeeded Henry II but died in 1199. Suddenly John Lackland had in his possession all of Britain.

He immediately started to destroy what he had. The laws of chivalry demanded that aristocrats captured in battle be ransomed and returned to their home country once the ransom was paid. John was having none of this. When he captured his nephew and rival, Arthur of Brittany, in 1202, he threatened the younger man with blinding and then had him thrown from a prison window – some even say it was John who pushed him. Twenty-two other aristocrats in Arthur's army were then placed in a castle and starved to death.

Starving became his favourite form of killing enemies – in one of the most notorious acts of his reign, he starved the wife and son of a former friend who he had fallen out with, William de Briouze.

In 1203, John was in the British-held Normandy when the King of France, Philip II, invaded. John did what was expected of him – he fled as quickly as possible, leaving his army to be slaughtered. He repeated the same trick in 1216 when the French army reached Kent in England – so rapid was his retreat that he was 10 miles from his army before they realized he was gone.

At a time of great bravery, such cowardice made him an object of ridicule, especially when compared to the "lionheartedness" of his brother Richard.

It was also a time of great chivalry in romance, but John failed in that department too, his lecherous behaviour around the wives and daughters of his friends and family causing no end of embarrassment. He married twice, his second wife being only nine years old. He had many mistresses and illegitimate children, not unheard of then, but contemporaries still saw his behaviour as extreme. As a chronicler of the time noted, "He lusted after beautiful women and because of this he shamed the high men of the land, for which reason he was greatly hated."

This hatred was not helped by the huge taxes he imposed on aristocrats across the land. Finally, in 1214, the barons had had enough. They rose against him, and so weak was John's position that he signed the Magna Carta, curtailing the Divine Right of Kings. From now on the king bowed to the government.

His end was, fittingly, an inglorious one – in 1216, he died of dysentery, presumably spending the last few days of his reign on the toilet suffering from stomach cramps, nausea, vomiting, fever and, of course, diarrhoea. No one was displeased to see him go.

It was in the sixteenth century that the legend of Robin Hood emerged, long after John's death. But when the storytellers were looking for the embodiment of evil to oppose Robin's goodness, they needed to look no further than a king who lost everything, all through his own stupidity and cruelty – King John.

IVAN THE TERRIBLE

He was born in 1530 "in the purple" – which means his father was king when he came into the world – but he spent his childhood in rags, neglected and abused. We know now that many a ruthless killer is the product of an abusive childhood, and when we look at the crimes of Ivan the Terrible it is hard not to think his cruel and pitiless acts were not some sort of revenge on a world that had treated him so brutally.

When Ivan was three, his father, Vasili the Grand Prince of Moscow, died, and he found himself prince, but he was under the control of two rival families vying for control of Russia, the Shuiskys and the Belskeys. Despite being their ruler, young Ivan was subjected to awful treatment, "brought up like vagrants and children of the poorest", he later wrote, adding, "What have I suffered for want of garments and food!"

His mother died when he was eight, and Ivan's behaviour started to deteriorate – he was known to torture animals, pulling the feathers out of live birds and throwing dogs and cats out of windows to their deaths.

ANCIENT MALEVOLENCE

It wasn't until he was 13 that he was able to take out his anger on humans rather than animals. Showing for the first time the ruthless streak which would one day lead to millions of deaths, Ivan accused the most powerful of the Shuiskys, Prince Andrei, of corruption. Andrei was arrested and put to death – some say Ivan had him torn to pieces by dogs.

At 16, in 1546, he was crowned Tsar of Russia and took a wife, Anastasia, who he is believed to have adored. The first few years of his reign were relatively peaceful, his cruelty kept in check while he was occupied by the demands of unifying Russian laws and government and redesigning Moscow. One of his commissions was St Basil's Cathedral, which some believe to be the most beautiful building in the world. Ivan certainly thought so, and he had the architect blinded so he could never design anything for anyone else.

Many believe it was the death of Anastasia in 1660 that tipped him into the mad violence which marked the last two decades of his reign and earned him the nickname "Terrible". He initially abdicated the throne, but he relented on the condition that he had a free hand to execute anyone he suspected of treason. This was agreed to. And all hell broke loose.

Ivan started the wholesale slaughter of anyone he even vaguely thought might be in a position to attack him, whether they had thought about it or not. Thousands of boyars – the Russian aristocracy – were killed, often by the "Oprichniki", a personal bodyguard which Ivan had created to carry out intimidation and mass executions. Some boyars were boiled alive, some were roasted over an open fire in front of their families, some were impaled. The slightest suspicion led to absolute carnage.

Ivan wasn't satisfied for long with only murdering the aristocrats. Soon the middle classes, shopkeepers and merchants felt his wrath. The Oprichniki began looting stores and burning down shops, usually killing the owners as well. The attacks were random and ruthless, and the population lived in fear of their village being targeted.

The poor were not spared either – Ivan's childhood suffering made him no more merciful to them than he had been to others. Many were killed, and others were evicted from the city, left to starve in the harsh Russian winters, joined by those who had seen their livelihoods destroyed by the Oprichniki.

An attack on the city of Novgorod, Moscow's most powerful rival, was perhaps his most vicious. He ordered an assault on the city in 1570. All the prominent members of the government and the clergy were rounded up, tortured and then burned to death on specially constructed frying pans. Their wives and children were drowned, being held under the icy water of the city's river by boat hooks and spears. In all, somewhere between 10,000 and 20,000 citizens of Novgorod were killed.

By then Ivan had brought all of Russia to its knees, mired in famine and poverty. But the final brutal act we know happened in his own home in 1581. Yelena, the wife of his second son, also called Ivan, was pregnant, and Ivan the Terrible grew angry at her for not dressing appropriately. His anger finally boiled over, and he beat her so severely that she miscarried. His son confronted him, and blows were exchanged – and the tsar killed his son with a hit to the head.

Three years later Ivan himself was dead, suffering a stroke while playing chess. Russia was finally rid of its tyrant, and much of the world rejoiced.

ATTILA THE HUN

They called him the "Scourge of God", and he was known for his greed and rapacity. As he laid waste to Europe, he spread terror in his wake, sparing no enemy in his pursuit of power. Nearly 2,000 years after his death, the name Attila the Hun resounds down the centuries as that of one of the most evil men in history.

He was born in 406 CE, one of two nephews of Rugila, leader of the Huns, a group of nomads living in Central Asia, the Caucasus and Eastern Europe that harried the Roman Empire in its dying days. On Rugila's death in 435 CE, both brothers assumed the throne.

The older brother, Bleda, was seen as the true ruler, and he negotiated a treaty with the Romans. Tall and good-looking, he is said to have kidnapped a Moor named Zerco and made him a court jester. Zerco made all the Huns laugh with his antics.

All except Attila, the younger brother, who was, according to the Roman diplomat Priscus, a man "of an irritable, blustering and truculent disposition" who had "a large head, deep-set eyes, flat nose and a thin beard". At the feast Priscus attended, everyone ate all that was on offer on ceramic plates – except Attila, who ate only meat from wooden plates like a barbarian, tearing it from the bones, which he threw over his shoulder.

Attila accepted being second in command for five years, but finally, enough was enough. He and Bleda were hunting together when Attila attacked. No one knows how Bleda was killed, but only one King of the Huns returned from the woods. From now on the evil, brutish Attila would be sole ruler. No more was seen of Zerco, either.

Attila ruled with an iron fist, feared by friends and enemies alike. He attacked the Roman Empire and its new capital, Constantinople, again and again, and rampaged through the Balkans, leaving a trail of desolation. Nations that obeyed strict rules of warfare were left devastated by the attacks of these "barbarian hordes".

Cities that were conquered were generally sacked, with as much loot as possible taken and added to the Huns' coffers. So devastated were the Romans that they were forced again and again to pay Attila to stop his attacks – on one occasion they agreed to pay him 2,100 pounds of gold to retreat from Constantinople, a staggering sum now, let alone then.

In 452, he attacked Italy, believing he had been promised the hand of Honoria, the sister of Valentinian III, emperor of Western Rome, and thus half of the king's territory. On being rebuffed, he swept across Valentinian's lands, destroying all crops and reducing Italy to famine.

Attila was finally halted at the legendary Battle of the Catalaunian Plains, one of the bloodiest conflicts in history. The Romans had formed an alliance with the Visigoths, and both fought against Attila and his troops. The battle shocked Europe with the level of carnage – Hydatius, a historian who lived at the time of Attila's invasion, reported the number of dead as 300,000, evenly divided between the combatants.

The battle was indecisive, but Attila was forced back. Undeterred, he attacked Italy the following year, but again he could make up no ground. Retiring to lick his wounds and plan another invasion, he also took as a new wife – he had many – the "beautiful young" Ildico.

It was on the night of the wedding that he met his death – and it was not the glorious one that he might have imagined. Getting drunk, he passed out in a stupor. The next morning his guards found his new bride weeping over his dead body. It seems that during the night he had suffered a nosebleed and choked to death on his own blood. The Scourge of God had gone to meet his maker.

According to Priscus, "They bound his coffins, the first with gold, the second with silver and the third with the strength of iron... iron because he subdued the nations, gold and silver because he received the honours of both empires." And those who made the coffins and who buried him were, as dictated by his will, also killed, "a dreadful pay for their labour".

KING HEROD

He is infamous for one act, which may not have in fact happened. But the mere fact that it is believed gives us an insight into how King Herod has gone down in history, whether or not he ordered the Massacre of the Innocents.

According to the Gospel of Matthew – the story appears nowhere else, not even in the other Gospels – Herod, the King of Judea since 37 BCE, was visited by the Three Wise Men who had witnessed the birth of Jesus and who told him a new King of Judea had been born in Bethlehem.

Herod angrily demanded that every child in the city under the age of two be murdered to make sure the "new king" did not grow up to take the throne. Warned of the impending massacre, Joseph and Mary fled to Egypt with baby Jesus. All the other children were killed.

Most historians have believed the story to be apocryphal. However, recent studies have suggested that the population of Bethlehem at the time would have only been about 300 people, which would usually equate to about 20 children under two. It was a massacre, but not a big enough one to appear in history books.

What the story does tell us is that Herod was generally regarded as the sort of man who would kill children. He had risen to power by overthrowing the ruling Hasmoneans and their king Antigonus in the Siege of Jerusalem. He had the king beheaded and 45 members of his retinue executed.

To consolidate his power, he set up a secret police force, cracking down on any dissent by whatever means necessary. To protect himself he also employed a bodyguard of 2,000 soldiers, well known for their brutality. He himself took particular delight in helping torture and kill those he regarded as enemies.

But it was the love of a woman that brought his downfall.

On ascending to the throne, Herod divorced his first wife, Doris, and married Mariamne, a Hasmonean. The marriage was initially in order to secure the throne, but he grew increasingly obsessed with his wife, said to be one of the great beauties of the time. He rarely let her out of his sight, and so terrified was he of her being with another man that when he went away from home, he gave strict orders that she be immediately killed if he failed to return.

Mariamne gradually became aware of the orders and reacted coldly to him the next time he returned. Herod's sister saw an opportunity to be rid of the more beautiful Mariamne and insinuated to her brother that his wife was plotting against him. Herod tortured Mariamne's servant, who knew of no plot but did know Mariamne was dissatisfied with Herod.

In a rage Herod ordered the death of his wife and 15 of her family. The moment it was done he realized his mistake and grieved for Mariamne, descending into madness and seeing visions of his dead wife everywhere. In a chilling echo of the massacre, legend has it that he had three of his sons executed to stop them from attempting to take the throne.

His own death was a terrible one – he caught a disease, known to posterity as "Herod's Evil", that led to his flesh putrefying, Such was the pain that he attempted suicide, but he was stopped by his cousin. But finally, in 4 BCE, he perished, his body wasted away to almost nothing.

He gave one final order. Terrified that he would not be mourned, he commanded that a large group of the most distinguished men in the kingdom come to Jericho, where he ruled, and then be killed so that the city would grieve, and he could make it seem to be for him.

The order was not carried out and, as expected, there were no mourners in Jericho when the world was finally free of the tyrant of Judea.

GILLES DE RAIS

We have already met Marquis de Sade, but before him was Gilles de Rais. For some, he is known as the world's first serial killer. The dispute is only about whether others preceded him, not about whether he can be defined as one.

Born in 1404, he was known during his lifetime for two things. First, he was one of France's greatest military heroes. Rais fought alongside Joan of Arc in 1429 at the Siege of Orléans and was awarded some of France's highest honours during the Hundred Years' War. He was made a Marshal of France, a rank given to generals of exceptional achievements.

But there was a darker side. Driven to excess, his immense appetites drove him to the edge of bankruptcy. His second fame rested on being an amateur playwright. He built himself his own theatre, producing his own play, *Le Mystère du Siège d'Orléans*, which he wrote himself and which featured 140 speaking parts and 500 extras, each of whom he had costumes handmade for, a new one for each performance. And every performance drove him deeper into debt.

Forced to sell off paintings, manuscripts from his immense library, even his clothes, he was arrested in 1440 after kidnapping a priest after a business dispute. It was then that the second thing he would become known for was revealed. Gilles de Rais was also a killer of children.

A dabbler in the occult, he built a chapel "for the bliss of his soul" in 1433. Where he sought bliss was not communion with God; it was in carrying out perverse acts with children, including the boys' choir of the chapel.

Children started disappearing from the areas around his holdings in the French city of Nantes. As it was not uncommon for the poor to give up their children to nobility like de Rais, nothing was thought of it for a long time. But some believe it was an open secret, as during his trial villagers reported seeing de Rais' servants carrying children out of his lands and burying them in mass graves.

It appears his first victim was a 12-year-old named Jeudon. The apprentice furrier was snatched by de Rais' cousins and accomplices and taken to the castle. Jeudon was dressed in finery and forced to imbibe an alcoholic drink of wine, sugar and spices. The boy was then taken up to a secret room and hung upside down, and the baron masturbated on him, then took him down and comforted him. Then the poor victim was cut to pieces with a short double-edged sword.

From then on, de Rais was unstoppable. It is believed around 140 boys and girls were killed by him in various ways similar to Jeudon, although the real number of deaths may have been much higher. All of them were used for perverse sex acts before they died. According to the cleric and alchemist François Prelati, who testified during the trial, the baron had attempted to summon demons to his castle. When the traditional methods had failed, he tried offering up the remnants of a dead child, ideally a fresh one.

We know little else about the trial – the details were so disturbing that even the court records were destroyed to avoid revealing the sickness that humanity is capable of – and this in a time of bloody and pitiless wars. We also know that under torture Gilles de Rais confessed to all of his crimes and that he was sentenced to be executed by simultaneous burning and hanging – one method of execution was not seen as sufficient.

On 26 October 1440, he and two accomplices were led to the place of execution. There he gave a pious speech to the huge crowd that had assembled. He was then hung from the neck over a funeral pyre. His burned remains were taken away for burial in an unmarked grave.

But human perversity did not end there. For more than a century after his death, parents in the area of Nantes commemorated his death by whipping their own children as punishment for their sins of the year. The children were told that this is what would have happened to them if Gilles de Rais was still alive.

But as we know, if he were, whipping would have been the least of it.

NERO

The Roman Empire was one of the greatest the world has ever known. Strong, confident, rich, it dominated the world in the early part of the Christian era. So it took quite a man to leave it in ruins. And the Emperor Nero was quite a man. It was said that he "fiddled while Rome burned" – that is to say that during the Great Fire of Rome in 64 CE, their emperor amused himself by playing on the lyre – but this may have been the least of his crimes.

He was born in 37 CE, and his mother Agrippina was the great-granddaughter of the first Roman emperor, Augustus. Nero's father died when he was three, and at 11, his mother married the then-emperor Claudius, who adopted the young boy as his own. When Claudius also died, the 17-year-old Nero became the emperor. Rome could not have known what it was letting itself in for.

A year earlier he had married his stepsister by Claudius, Octavia, at his mother's behest. Agrippina now had both her son and her stepdaughter in charge of Rome and had positioned herself to be the power behind the throne. Nero, however, had other plans.

No one is absolutely sure how Nero killed his mother, but no one doubts that he did. In some versions he poisoned her, in others he stabbed her in the womb from which he had been born. The most common tale is that he sent her to sea in a boat he had designed to sink. Whichever is true, Nero was now the sole power in Rome, although he did also poison to death his stepbrother, Britannicus, to be on the safe side.

His was a life of excess – the image we have of Roman emperors lying about eating grapes and taking women to bed comes from him, although he was far from a layabout. His affairs were prodigious, and his wife Claudia suffered terribly. He again came up with a solution – he first sent Claudia into exile, and then he had her murdered. Her veins were cut to make it look like suicide, but as she failed to die, the murderers simply cut her head off. This they delivered to Nero and his lover, Poppaea.

Nero then married Poppaea and was with her for three years. They had a daughter together, Claudia Augusta, who died at five months old. Poppaea's failure to have another child angered Nero, and she went the same way as his mother and first wife, although this time his method was less sophisticated – he simply kicked her to death in 65 CE.

He took up with the woman who was to be his next wife, Statilia Messalina, almost immediately. She was already married to Nero's friend Vestinus, so the emperor ordered him to commit suicide so she would be free. Faced with little choice, Vestinus did so.

But one wife was no longer enough, and besides, he missed Poppaea. Nero came up with an ingenious – and evil – solution. He noticed that one of his slave boys bore an uncanny resemblance to Poppaea. So he had the boy castrated and then married him, making him wear her clothes, calling the boy by her name and raping him nightly.

He then decided that he also wanted a husband and married a man named Doryphorus. Nero wore a bridal veil and imitated a virgin being taken by force as Doryphorus consummated the marriage. An orgy was then ordered, with men allowed to take any woman they wanted, and women not allowed to say no. According to legend, a number of slaves were tied to stakes around the grounds, and Nero, covered with skins of wild animals, was let loose from a cage and attacked their genitals.

So much for his home life. In public he was equally cruel and malicious – contemporary accounts say that he was driven by bloodlust and delighted in the deaths of slaves, holding magnificent events at which they would be slaughtered. He also enjoyed persecuting Christians – the prophets Peter and Paul were killed on his watch. When the Great Fire of Rome broke out, which some believe he himself may have lit, he blamed Christians and was delighted when they were punished – many were starved to death, burned, fed to lions, crucified, torn apart by dogs, used as torches and nailed to crosses. Some came to regard him as the Antichrist.

The Great Fire saw popular support suddenly drain from Nero. Rumours that he started the fire in order to clear the way for a new palace spread throughout the citizens, and armies were raised against him. Realizing he would lose, he decided that he would kill himself, but he lost his nerve. He forced a few of his remaining compatriots to kill themselves so he could see what it was like, then finally he forced his secretary to kill him after failing to drive the knife into himself. His last words were, "What an artist the world is losing!"

Nero had taken a prosperous empire and fatally wounded it – never again would Rome be so dominant. His likeness was removed from paintings and statues, his name erased from books and his ashes thrown to the wind. But, like his uncle Caligula, he remains a byword for debauchery, sexual excess – and just plain evil.

TYRANTS AND DICTATORS

"L'État, c'est moi" – *"The State is me."* So declared King Louis XIV of France in the seventeenth century. Absolute power has been the dream of many rulers throughout history, but since the start of the twentieth century, the possibility for absolute dictatorship has increased in ways Louis could only have dreamed of. Ever more powerful weapons, ever more destructive methods of punishment and death, and ever greater systems of surveillance have meant that a ruler of malevolence has all the levers he could need to hold an entire nation in the palm of his hand.

The number of deaths in the following pages sometimes beggars description – 15 million, 30 million, 65 million. The latter figure, the dead ascribed to Mao Zedong, would be one in six of the Earth's population in Louis' time. Even in today's world it is roughly the population of France.

Some dictators had fewer people to play with but did their evil best. They left trails of destruction, annihilating whole communities with the stroke of a pen. Husbands, wives, children, sons, daughters, lovers, mothers and fathers. Gone in some insane desire for domination. And yet no man among them ever became the god he desired to be – the death of many of these tyrants is as inglorious as their murders.

So as you read on, remember, each death here is a tragedy, and each death represents only a small percentage of the havoc wreaked by men who chose evil over the possibility of good.

ADOLF HITLER

There is no way to get around him. Has there been a more evil man in human history? It is possible that if some who came before him had access to the planes, the bombs and the gas chambers they may have matched his crimes, but they didn't, and so Adolf Hitler stands out as the man who has almost certainly caused the most human suffering and misery.

His story is well known but loses no horror in the telling. Born in Austria in 1889, he served Germany in the First World War, receiving an Iron Cross for his bravery. When Germany surrendered, he joined a huge part of the population in being angry at his rulers for their capitulation. But he had one particular talent, which was using that anger to drive him forward to a position where he could carry out a programme of destruction on a scale never seen before.

In the 1920s, he found himself in prison, arrested for high treason when his new political party – the far-right Nazi Party – attempted a coup. In prison, he wrote a book which would set out his political ambitions and general world view – *Mein Kampf*, which translates as *My Struggle*. Germany was to be returned to greatness, retaking the lands it had lost in the First

World War. And, he argued, a cancer was to be removed from the German blood: the Jew.

If only one of Hitler's barbaric crimes had occurred, it would have been enough. Elected Chancellor of Germany in 1933 – he would call himself the Führer, meaning leader – for the next 12 years, he would carry out the systematic purging of Germany and much of Europe of what he and the Nazis called the "Jewish Menace". Some 6 million Jews were sent to their deaths, most of them in specially constructed gas chambers. Jewish men, women and children were driven into the chambers, and Zyklon B was pumped into the rooms, causing a hideous death. The bodies, usually emaciated by long-term imprisonment in concentration camps, were then dumped in mass graves. The Holocaust remains the greatest crime in the whole of the bloody twentieth century – perhaps in all human history.

But Hitler's crimes didn't stop there. His attempts to establish a Greater Germany saw him declare war on most surrounding countries, and the battles led to millions of deaths – the Battle of Stalingrad, his attempt to annex Russia, resulted in a death toll of 1.2 million people. The war dead of the Second World War included over 50 million who died in battle – the vast majority due to Hitler's ambitions.

Closer to home, he created a state which lived in fear – not only Jews but gay people and those with disabilities were executed for the "health" of the German people. His police force, the Gestapo, was responsible for thousands of deaths of anyone considered suspect – and the dead were often the lucky ones. Stories of torture are horrifying in their details, and if Hitler was not actually in attendance at most, the Gestapo were still well aware of what his requirements were.

No one was safe. One of his first acts as Führer was to burn down the German government building, the Reichstag, and declare a Third Reich, which would "rule for 1,000 years". Then, in 1934, he oversaw what is known as "The Night of the Long Knives", when he purged the Nazi Party of members he either suspected of disloyalty or who he thought were capable of it. The estimated deaths were between 700 and 1,000, a small number compared to his later crimes, but it was still a death toll that sent shockwaves through Europe.

In 1935, he enacted the Nuremberg Laws, denying Jewish people citizenship and prohibiting marriage or sexual relations with people of "German or related blood". This was the first step in what the laws called the "Final Solution" of the "Jewish problem".

Then, in 1938, he invaded Austria and Czechoslovakia, claiming them for Germany. The world attempted to negotiate with him, signing peace treaties, which Hitler then ignored. On 1 September 1939, he invaded Poland, no part of which he could claim had ever been German. Attempts at appeasement were over. The Second World War began two days later, on 3 September. For the next two years, Germany held the upper hand, with their blitzkrieg tactics cutting a swathe through Europe, right up to the doorstep of the United Kingdom. But Hitler shared two characteristics of evil men that led to their doom. The first was hubris, the feeling that one cannot be defeated. His attack on Russia in 1942 stretched his army across two fronts and caused its decimation.

The second was that he was completely self-absorbed, and the iron fist with which he had ruled Germany gradually loosened. As we shall see, this allowed many men to carry out their own evil deeds, but it also made his tactics chaotic and unsustainable. He spent much of the second half of the war sleeping in until the afternoon and watching his own propaganda films at his holiday retreat.

By 1945, it was all over. His death was as inglorious as it should have been. The day before he killed himself, he married his lover, Eva Braun, in the bunker into which he had retreated, and then, on 30 April, the pair bit into vials of cyanide. Hitler then shot himself in the head – he was the last victim of his own reign of terror.

The results of Hitler's actions continue to shape the world today. For the Jewish people in particular, the genocide left few untouched, and the Holocaust has become a defining part of their story. One man's evil can spread outward, and Hitler's drew in more than anyone else's ever has.

JOSEPH STALIN

"One death is a tragedy, a million deaths a statistic." So said Joseph Stalin, leader of the Soviet Union from 1924 until his death in 1953. Accounts vary on how many people became statistics due to Stalin, but most estimates put it at around 40 million. Like Hitler, many of the casualties were war dead. But in the case of Stalin, his own citizens accounted for a much higher number.

He was born in 1878 and named Besarionis dze Jughashvili (Stalin, meaning "Man of Steel", was a name he adopted in 1912). His first calling was to be a priest, and he joined a seminary as a teenager. There he had his first access to books and became a voracious reader. The books that had the greatest effect on him were those written by Karl Marx, and by the age of 20, he declared himself a Marxist. He left the school a year later and became involved in revolutionary causes.

By 1901, he had joined the Bolshevik Party, espousing the establishment of a Marxist worker's state in Russia. The party had been started by the charismatic revolutionary, Vladimir Lenin. Stalin met him in 1905, and for the next 12 years, they were part of a group attempting to overthrow the Tsar of

Russia, Nicholas II. Their success in 1917 saw Lenin become Premier of Russia, which was then renamed the USSR. Stalin was editor of the Bolshevik newspaper *Pravda* (meaning *Truth*). By 1922, he had risen to become General Secretary of the Party, a position which became that of supreme leader on Lenin's death in 1924.

Few could have guessed that a man who was seen as one of the less brilliant of the revolutionaries would become one of the great tyrants of the twentieth century – in fact, of any century.

The first years of Soviet rule had seen a cultural and artistic flowering, as citizens tested the new way of living. Stalin soon put paid to that. As General Secretary, he saw his role as taking complete control of all aspects of Soviet life. Anyone who was suspected of not being "pure" in their devotion to communism – or "pure" in their devotion to Stalin – was eliminated. Stalin instituted a vast number of "show trials" – those accused of treachery were arrested, tortured and then made to confess their sins. They were then executed.

Stalin also took control of the economy. Marx's motto, "From each according to his abilities, to each according to his needs", was perverted by the goal of a planned economy, which led to disastrous famines. As long as the market targets were met, the number of people who died in labour or starved to death was immaterial. Statistics, just statistics.

His dictatorship was made effective by his secret police, the notorious NKVD. No one was safe, and the NKVD's grip on the population was so complete that citizens became their own police force – people lived in fear of being denounced for any criticism of Stalin, even in the "privacy" of their own homes. A police state became a terror state, as more and more of the

Soviet people were taken from their homes on the basis of rumour and gossip.

Many of them were sent to the "Gulag", a prison system Lenin set up in 1919. These were forced labour camps, set up in the remote wilderness of places like Siberia, where those accused of treachery who had not been executed were sent into a living hell. Under Stalin's watch, the population held in the Gulag had reached around 100,000 in the late 1920s; by 1940, some 1.5 million were held in the camps. The total number believed to have spent time in the Gulag is 14 million, although some estimates put it at 20 million.

There the prisoners were subjected to torture, starvation and humiliation. This was called re-education, and those who were able to convince the authorities of their allegiance to Stalin might be set free. Nearly 2 million were unable to convince the authorities, and so perished in the camps.

Stalin's elimination of those he regarded as suspect reached its peak in 1937 when he organized what has become known as the Great Purge. Anyone suspected of being an enemy of Stalin was executed, which included many of the highest-ranking officials in the Soviet Union, who had stood alongside both Lenin and Stalin throughout the revolution. Another 2 million men, women and children were added to Stalin's pile of corpses. He even killed the heads of the NKVD, who had worked with him to carry out the purge.

In the Second World War, the Soviet Union became crucial in the battle against Adolf Hitler's Germans, and Stalin was seen by many in the West as part of the alliance that stopped the Nazis. But at what cost? The Battle of Stalingrad has gone down as one of the most horrific battles in world history, as two armies, led by men with no regard for human life, faced off against each other. Both were willing to sacrifice their own soldiers in the pursuit of victory. And victory meant imposing their regimes of terror on all of Europe. The losses on both sides were in the millions.

Stalin's reign of terror lasted for another eight years after the end of the Second World War. His police state moved south to embrace the countries of Eastern Europe. As Winston Churchill put it, an Iron Curtain had been drawn across Europe. The famines also spread. Meanwhile, Stalin's own health declined, although any doctors who suggested he was dying were executed.

On 6 March 1953, he died. As per his instructions, those who celebrated his death were rounded up and killed. But many celebrated in secret. One of the most evil men in history was dead. And it was no tragedy.

SADDAM HUSSEIN

One of the most powerful weapons any tyrant has is what is known as the "cult of personality". Those who follow the leader come to identify with them, worship them and see anyone who is not a follower as an apostate – one who has failed to believe in a god. For almost four decades, Saddam Hussein was a god, ruling over Iraq with an iron fist. Those who opposed him were killed. Those who did not follow him met the same fate.

His birth in 1937 was ill-omened. His father died before he was born, and his mother, consumed by grief, tried to kill herself and the baby inside her. She failed, and her newborn was named Saddam, meaning "the fighter who stands steadfast".

At ten, he fled home and went to live with an uncle in Baghdad. By the time he was 21, he was heavily involved in revolutionary politics, joining the Ba'ath, which sought to overthrow the government of Iraq. When he joined there were only 300 members, and only 1,000 when he was part of an attempt to assassinate the prime minister.

It was not until 1968 that a coup saw the Ba'ath take control of Iraq. Ahmed Hassan al-Bakr became president and appointed Saddam as vice-president. For 11 years, Saddam bided his time. In 1979, al-Bakr stood down. At 42 years of age, Saddam Hussein became president of Iraq. And unleashed a terror seldom seen in world history.

He himself instigated the cult of personality – his image was put up in every school and government building in Iraq. Dissenters were publicly shamed and then killed. There was no official opposition to Saddam Hussein, nor was there an unofficial one. He was the supreme leader, and everyone was forced to bow down to him.

One of his first acts as president was to invade neighbouring Iran. The war lasted eight years and saw a million casualties. It ended in a stalemate – not one death achieved anything. He then took revenge on rural Kurds on his own border who had sided with Iran, an attack recognized by Human Rights Watch as an act of genocide – the intentional destruction of a people. Estimates vary, but it is believed over 100,000 Kurds were killed.

Soon after, he invaded Kuwait, leading to the Gulf War of 1990–91, in which Iraq was completely defeated at the cost of 35,000 lives. Asked for his motivation, he responded, "When I get something into my head I act. That's just the way I am."

But it was what he did to his own country that made Saddam one of the most evil men in history and which earned him the nickname "The Butcher of Baghdad". It is estimated that nearly 300,000 Iraqis died at the hands of his regime, and most of the deaths were after a regime of terror and torture, the likes of which have been seldom seen.

Iraq became a state completely under the thumb of Saddam Hussein. The country choked under the yoke of authoritarianism, with any dissenting opinions likely to lead to a death sentence. The use of torture was part of basic policing, and suspects were treated to appalling brutality and deprivation.

During his reign he held two elections for the position of president, winning the first time with 99.96 per cent of the vote and the second time with 100 per cent – on a turnout that was also 100 per cent! According to his regime, every one of the 11.5 million eligible voters had cast their ballot for Saddam. Unsurprisingly, foreign observers declared these elections rigged.

The US president, George W. Bush, described Iraq as part of an Axis of Evil, which included Iran and North Korea. He also authorized the invasion of Iraq in March 2003 with the express intention of overthrowing the dictator. With US forces closing in, Saddam fled, and televisions showed the Iraqi population toppling his statue in Baghdad's Firdos Square.

The pursuit of Saddam Hussein would last many months and include the deaths of his sons, Uday and Qusay – both known for their own violent, ruthless personalities – and his 14-year-old grandson, Mustafa.

On 13 December 2003, in Operation Red Dawn, Saddam was captured by American forces. He was found hiding in a hole in the city of Tikrit, 140 kilometres (87 miles) northwest of Baghdad. In July 2004, he stood trial, charged with the murder of 148 people, the torture of women and children, and the illegal arrest of 399 other people, a small percentage of the thousands and thousands who had suffered at his hand. On 5 November 2006, he was found guilty and sentenced to death.

On 30 December 2006, Iraq was finally rid of Saddam Hussein. Despite his request that he be shot by firing squad in recognition of his military status, Saddam was hung by the neck like a common criminal – his neck broke as the trapdoor opened and the rope dropped him. According to some accounts, his corpse was then stabbed six times, before he was buried in a family tomb.

The tomb was destroyed soon after by angry Iraqis, and the body of the Butcher of Baghdad was taken away – whereabouts unknown.

KIM JONG IL

We have all seen the footage – hundreds of soldiers, male and female, marching in exact time with each other, with exactly the same expressions. It inspires awe and fear, and not a little sympathy. This is the army of North Korea, just one expression of the total control the State has over its people. It is one thing to take physical control of a population, to kill and injure them, but to take control of minds on this scale takes a special type of evil. It can be hard to decide between him, his father and his son, but it is Kim Jong Il who seems to have perfected this level of brutality and mind control.

It was Kim's father, Kim Il Sung, who established North Korea as a totalitarian state when he ascended to power in 1966. In the 1960s, North Korea had a slightly higher standard of living than the South, but Kim Il Sung would change all that. Establishing close ties with the Soviet Union, he set up a personality cult on a scale that is virtually unprecedented. Calling himself "Great Leader", he erected statues of himself throughout North Korea, and his portrait appeared everywhere.

He also set up a three-level caste system, with "core", "wavering" or "hostile" classes. Which class you belonged to dictated where you lived, what you could do, whether you could receive education or employment and who you could associate with or marry. Those in the hostile class, which included intellectuals, landowners and those of other political affiliations than the Great Leader, were killed, exiled or placed in prison.

On his death on 7 July 1994, his son Kim Jong Il ascended not only to being president but to the official rank of President for Life. Any hopes that Kim would be less of a dictator than his father were soon dashed. The younger Kim turned out to be even more repressive than his father. He may have called himself Dear Leader rather than Great Leader, but he was no less convinced of his supremacy.

Born in 1941, it is believed he was educated in China. Joining the Workers' Party in 1961, he rose up the ranks. But when his father took power in 1966, Kim, then 25, had no further need to work his way up anywhere. He decided to become a filmmaker while waiting to succeed his father as president. His task was to ensure loyalty and to continue his father's cult of personality by making films glorifying him.

His political activities continued, and in 1991, he was named Supreme Commander of the Korean People's Army. He also took charge of many internal affairs. Three years later he became Supreme Leader. He set a period of mourning for his father and immediately cracked down on any dissent. We can never be sure how many North Koreans died then or since, but the measures he enacted were ruthless. There were, in North Korea, no second chances. By 2004, according to Human Rights Watch, there were 200,000 political prisoners. And for those outside prison, "Virtually every aspect of political, social and economic life is controlled by the government." Citizenship and therefore rights depended, Kim stated, on ideology, not birth. Support Kim or lose every human right and possibly life itself.

Meanwhile, he turned out to be economically incompetent, leading his population into severe famine. The fall of the Soviet Union meant less financial support to prop up the government, and millions were forced into poverty. In addition, Kim concentrated a huge percentage of government spending on the military – those big parades – at the expense of feeding his population. He also had at least 17 palaces to pay the upkeep on.

But any thought of protesting these injustices was immediately quashed by the threat of violence, imprisonment, exile or death. The cult of personality that had been created around his father grew even greater around Kim – a "thought crime" against Kim was as severely punished as an actual act of resistance. People could be denounced by anyone, any time. A climate of fear invaded every aspect of North Korean life.

It was not only his own population that had reason to fear him. Some believe he was responsible for the bombing of a South Korean plane in 1987, which killed 115 people, and for the murder by bombing of 17 South Korean officials while on a visit to Burma in 1983. He has also been accused of chemical weapon attacks across the border and working on creating a nuclear arsenal. However, no evidence has been obtained to back these claims up.

It was in 2008 that his health started to fail. For a while, the regime kept up the pretence of the Dear Leader being in good health, publishing photographs of him visiting hospitals and factories and attending parades, but it was believed outside North Korea that he had suffered a stroke and that many of the photographs were of a lookalike stand-in.

Speculation grew about who would follow Kim to the presidency when he died. His eldest son, Kim Yong Hyun, would have ascended, but he fell out of favour after being arrested in Japan, attempting to visit Tokyo Disneyland! On 2 June 2007, it was announced that Kim's youngest son, Kim Jong Un, would be the next president, taking the name "The Brilliant Comrade".

On 17 December 2011, Kim Jong Il suffered a heart attack while travelling by train (he had a fear of flying). His body was preserved and displayed at the capital Pyongyang's Kumsusan Palace of the Sun. His birthday of 16 February was declared "the greatest auspicious holiday of the nation" – celebrated each year, forever.

MENGISTU HAILE MARIAM

The Holocaust represented a terrible awakening for the world. The fact that an attempt could be made to wipe an entire group of people from the Earth demonstrated that international laws were not fit for purpose.

So in 1948, three years after the Second World War, the United Nations Genocide Convention came up with a definition of genocide which could be applied against tyrants and dictators like Hitler. It defined genocide as any of five "acts committed with intent to destroy, in whole or in part, a national, ethnical, racial or religious group".

These five acts were: killing members of the group, imposing living conditions intended to destroy the group, causing group members serious bodily or mental harm, forcibly transferring children out of the group and preventing births. These are all methods by which an attempt could be made to eliminate an entire ethnicity.

It took a 12-year trial, but in 2007, Mengistu Haile Mariam, the former president of Ethiopia, was convicted of genocide and given a life sentence, later upgraded on appeal to a death sentence. The verdict was reached in absentia – Mengistu had fled to Zimbabwe in 1991 after his regime was toppled. The overthrow of Mengistu brought to an end one of the bloodiest eras not only in Ethiopian history but in the entire world.

Mengistu was born in 1937 when Ethiopia was ruled by Italy, and it is said that his parents were slaves. When the Italians were defeated in 1941, his father joined the army of the emperor Haile Selassie, and the young Mengistu spent his childhood in army camps. He was expelled from school and so joined the army itself at an early age, gradually rising through the ranks.

He was known for his quick temper and his hatred of the US. He also hated the upper classes of Ethiopia and became a convert to Marxist-Leninism. In 1974, he joined the Derg, a Marxist-Leninist military junta that sought to impose a communist state on Ethiopia.

That same year, the emperor Haile Selassie, now in his eighties, was forced from power by the Derg – the emperor was in a weakened political situation when the revolutionaries attacked. His fall saw the end of an empire that stretched back to the thirteenth century.

Mengistu used his considerable political skill to outmanoeuvre other members of the Derg, becoming deputy chairman in 1975 and then supreme leader of Ethiopia in 1977. Before that, in 1974, he was responsible for the execution of 61 ex-officials of the Imperial government and the death of the Patriarch of the Ethiopian Orthodox Church, Abune Theophilos, who was strangled by an electrical wire.

But it was one other death which would cement Mengistu's position as the head of the Derg. The former emperor, Haile

Selassie, one of the greatest of all Ethiopian rulers (and, as Prince Ras Tafari, the God of the Rastafarians), was killed in his bed – it is believed Mengistu pressed a pillow to his face. The son of a slave now had complete power.

He used this power for evil. Estimates place the number of Ethiopian deaths under his regime at somewhere between 500,000 and 2 million. Many died due to the 1983–85 famine, which inspired Live Aid, but which was caused by Mengistu's policies. All farms had been nationalized and farmers compelled to join collective farms. All agricultural products were no longer to be offered on the free market but were to be controlled and distributed by the government. It was a disaster, and Mengistu covered it up.

But it was not just his policies which led to thousands of deaths; it was also his police. Soon after the revolution, Mengistu declared war on counter-revolutionaries and set up militias to kill them. This was well-organized – local committees would meet to draft lists of suspects who would be killed and their bodies taken away. Family members had to pay to have the corpses returned. So precise were the documents generated in carrying out these killings that they became a large part of the evidence in Mengistu's trial.

It is estimated hundreds of thousands of adults died this way. Children were not safe either. The Save the Children Fund, in one report, stated that "a thousand children have been killed, and their bodies are left in the streets and are being eaten by wild hyenas." It added, "You can see the heaped-up bodies of murdered children, most of them aged 11 to 13, lying in the gutter."

Ethiopians were now living in a police state, where the smallest suspicion could lead to execution. But Mengistu was losing his grip on power as the Soviet Union, facing its own demise, withdrew support in 1990, cutting off the main source of Mengistu's funds. In May 1991, rebel forces advanced on the capital, Addis Ababa. Mengistu fled and found asylum in Zimbabwe, with his friend Robert Mugabe.

He has never returned to Ethiopia, and if he did, he would be executed. It is said that he lives in luxury, without a care for those he killed. There is always some evil that will not face justice. It seems likely Mengistu Haile Mariam will only face his if there is a next world.

IDI AMIN

He was president of Uganda for only eight years, and yet Idi Amin will go down as one of the most brutal dictators in world history. From 1971, when he took power in a coup, to 1979, when the army of neighbouring Tanzania, helped by a large percentage of the Ugandan population, brought him down, Amin ran a ruthless police state. We will never know for sure how many were killed by his regime, but Amnesty International puts the figure at around half a million. In eight years!

The list of his crimes incorporates political repression, extrajudicial killings and human rights violations on an unprecedented scale. His was a corrupt and nepotistic regime, and his economic mismanagement drove huge swathes of his population into poverty and starvation. By the end of the 1970s, the name Idi Amin stood for the worst type of military dictatorship.

He was born in 1928 to a Uganda ruled by Britain, and his father had been forcibly conscripted into the British King's African Rifles. Amin was to follow in 1946, first working as a cook. He was promoted through the ranks, eventually reaching the highest rank a Black soldier could attain in the army.

Known as charismatic and a leader who showed his enemies no mercy, he was an imposing figure who stood 1.93 m (6 ft 4 in.) tall. Powerfully built, he was the Ugandan light heavyweight boxing champion from 1951 to 1960. He was also a fine swimmer and rugby player. But he had far greater ambitions.

When Uganda became independent in 1961, he rose further in the ranks, and by 1970, he was commander of the entire Ugandan army under the president, Milton Obote. But Amin didn't like to be under any leader. In 1971, when Obote was in Singapore on a state visit, Amin seized power. He was greeted as a hero and promised to hold elections as soon as possible and to release all political prisoners incarcerated by Obote. His was, he said, a caretaker government.

The elections never came. Within a week he had declared himself president, and he began imposing military law on Uganda. The constitution was suspended. Obote tried to organize a counter-revolution from Tanzania but failed. The chief justice, Kagimu Kiwanuka, was arrested and then killed in his chambers. The Archbishop, Janani Luwum, was killed in a fake car accident. And those prisoners he did release immediately became part of his brutal police force, which carried out their killings with a sadism matching that of their leader.

He also began a programme of ethnic cleansing focused on the Christian tribes such as the Acholi and Langi. Their soldiers were massacred. In one particularly brutal instance, 32 officers were crammed into a cell, which was then dynamited. There were no survivors.

Amin also attacked Uganda's Asian population, who had come to Uganda when it was a British colony. Those who were not killed were forcibly expelled, some 60,000 of them. This had a disastrous effect on the Ugandan economy – around 90 per cent of the taxes paid to the government were paid by the Asian population. The economy collapsed and would not recover under Amin.

In 1976, he declared himself president for life. In June the same year, he was personally involved in hijacking a French airliner flying from Israel to France. The hijackers landed at Entebbe in Uganda, keeping 103 Jewish passengers on the plane and demanding the release of 53 militants imprisoned in Israel, Kenya, West Germany and elsewhere. Israel attacked the airport, freeing all the hostages except three and killing the hijackers. One Israeli soldier was killed, Yonatan Netanyahu, brother of future Israeli president Benjamin. In retaliation for Kenya's assistance in the raid, Amin also ordered the killing of hundreds of Kenyans living in Uganda.

His behaviour grew increasingly erratic – his mood swings became legendary, and he was known to suddenly lash out at his closest comrades, sending them to death on a whim. He played up to Western caricatures that accused him of cannibalism, boasting he kept the severed heads of enemies in a freezer.

His sexual appetites were known to be colossal – aside from his six wives, his mistresses were too numerous to count. He married two wives in 1966, one in 1967 and one in 1972, divorcing three of the four in 1974 – one was subsequently beheaded, and one arrested. In 1975, he married a 19-year-old go-go dancer, whose previous boyfriend then disappeared, rumoured to have been beheaded. Amin is believed to have fathered around 60 children.

But by the late 1970s, his grip on power was beginning to slip as Ugandans continued to suffer from the ongoing economic disasters he inflicted on them. A subsequent failed invasion of Tanzania left his position fatally weakened. His army met defeat after defeat, and so desperate was Amin that he challenged the Tanzanian president Julius Nyerere to a boxing match to settle the war. Nyerere ignored him and pressed for victory. On 11 April 1979, Nyerere's forces captured the Ugandan capital, Kampala, and Amin fled by helicopter.

He spent the last 24 years of his life living in exile in Saudi Arabia, unrepentant for his brutal despotism. When he was hospitalized with liver failure, his family requested he be brought back to Uganda to die. The Ugandan president Yoweri Museveni was blunt: if he came back, he would face trial, whatever the state of his health. His family turned off life support in July 2003, and he was buried in a simple grave in Saudi Arabia, where few, if any, people visit him.

MAO ZEDONG

For some, he remains an inspiration, the man who set up China to become a world superpower and a beacon of socialism. But the numbers don't lie. Ask any search engine which person has been responsible for the most deaths in history, and there is always one answer. Mao Zedong. And the number of deaths? A staggering 65 million.

As Stalin taught us, it can be easy to regard these murders, like all of those in this book, as just a statistic. But every one of those deaths was someone with hopes and dreams, a family that cared for them and with unlimited potential. Each human being is a world. Directly or indirectly, Mao snuffed out 65 million different worlds in the pursuit of an impossible ideal – a communist state where all were equal. He did make many equal – they were all dead.

Remarkably, 45 million of these deaths occurred in just four years between 1958 and 1962. This was named The Great Leap Forward, during which Mao, who had become Chairman of the Chinese Communist Party and therefore leader of China in 1949, attempted to change China from an agrarian society into an industrial one. This is a change that has taken hundreds of years in other countries. Mao wanted it done as quickly as possible, whatever the consequences. And the consequences were terrible.

There were many complex factors, but the main cause is simple. Private farming was abolished, forced labour was introduced and quotas for production were set by the central government. Communities that failed to meet these quotas faced brutal punishments. As any farmer will tell you, in agriculture there are good years and bad years – setting a quota is madness. Terrified of being punished, local leaders exaggerated the sizes of their crops, leading to a huge overestimation of food availability. Meanwhile, crops were failing due to the impossibility of Mao's methods of farming. People were left to starve as production fell dramatically. Mao had engineered the greatest famine in human history. Rural China became a hell on Earth.

At first, the scale of the damage was, it was later argued, hidden from Mao – bad weather was blamed for crop failure. But as the devastation became increasingly impossible to ignore, Mao doubled down on reshaping the countryside, blaming political opponents for sabotaging his plans, and jailing and executing enormous numbers of what he called "rightists". Projects such as the Banqiao Dam were initiated – large dams intended to change water patterns throughout China. So shoddily made were these dams that 62 of them collapsed in 1975, leading to thousands and perhaps millions more deaths – Banqiao alone saw another 240,000 die.

So who was Chairman Mao? The son of a peasant, he was born in 1893 in Hunan. His father was strict and regularly beat Mao and his siblings. His mother, a Buddhist, attempted to intervene when she could but also suffered physical violence.

Perhaps Mao was already becoming immune to the effects of physical suffering.

A voracious reader, Mao soon became involved in revolutionary activities and, in 1911, an actual revolution, which ended the 300-year-old Qing dynasty and established the Republic of China. Mao spent six months as a soldier in the Revolutionary Army.

Demobbed in 1912, he drifted through a series of jobs, before studying to be a teacher. At university he again involved himself in politics, becoming more and more radical. In 1921, after graduation, he helped set up the Chinese Communist Party, rising through the ranks and participating in a number of protests and uprisings against the Nationalist government.

Most important was the 1934–35 Long March, during which Mao led the First Red Army more than 9,000 kilometres (5,600 miles) to join up with other forces to continue their battle against the Nationalists. It won Mao great prestige. By 1943, he was in charge of the entire Party. And, on 1 October 1949, when the Communist Party finally claimed victory, he became the leader of the whole country.

He immediately cracked down on dissidents – as many as 800,000 were killed in the counter-revolutionary campaign, while in the first two years, another million were killed in the first wave of land reform. Next, in every village, landlords were publicly executed as an example of the evils of private property. Another 2–5 million lost their lives due to this. Finally, perhaps as many as 4–6 million people were sent to "reform through labour" camps, where many perished. Then came The Great Leap Forward and the 45 million dead.

The rest of Mao's reign continued in the same way, although without repeating such a huge mass murder. Unbeknown to him, Mao was also killing himself – a life-long chain smoker, he suffered heart and lung disease throughout the 1970s, and on 9 September 1976, he suffered his third and final heart attack. One million people filed past his coffin, and his body was then transferred to the Mausoleum of Mao Zedong, where it remains, encased in glass.

The Communist Party of China has since officially reviewed his legacy and regards it as 70 per cent good and 30 per cent bad for China. Small mercy for the 65 million dead.

KING LEOPOLD II

It was called the Congo Free State, but never has the name of a nation been less appropriate. From 1885 to 1908, the place that would later become the Democratic Republic of Congo was not so much a nation as a slave farm, literally owned by the king of Belgium, Leopold II. For those 23 years, he committed crimes against humanity as severe as any that have occurred in human history. He did it entirely for profit, and the profit he made was immense.

Situated in Central Africa, the Congo had been too remote for much European interest or influence until the mid-nineteenth century – only Portugal had paid much attention. That changed on 5 February 1885. Leopold convinced other European powers that he wanted to bring "civilization" to the Congolese, and his mission was a charitable one. He also told them he would not put any tax on trade with the region, especially its valuable rubber plantations. All he asked for was a free hand.

In a time when the European powers were engaged in what became known as the "Scramble for Africa" – between 1870 and 1885, the amount of Africa under European control went from 10 to 90 per cent – Leopold's wish was granted. But unlike the other powers in other parts of Africa, Leopold did not establish a colony. Instead, he literally "bought" the Congo, paying the other European powers for possession of it. It became his own personal belonging.

What followed was one of the bloodiest eras in the history of Western domination of Africa. While still pretending to be humanitarian, Leopold ruled the Congo Free State as his own personal forced labour camp, enriching himself with both rubber and ivory. It is estimated that almost half the population, some 10 million people, died of punishment and malnutrition during his 23-year reign, but that figure may be even higher.

For many, death was preferable to continuing to live under such a brutal regime. Notoriously, Leopold employed other Congolese to enforce his rule, and they were given free rein to ensure that his quotas were met. Any workers who failed to reach his productivity targets – and this included men, women, children and, on occasion, whole villages – would either be killed or have their hands and, sometimes, feet amputated.

Leopold also allowed the kidnapping of wives and children as an "incentive" for workers. Only when they had met their quota would their family be returned, and inevitably many of those who returned had been subjected to sexual assault and torture while in captivity.

The squads that Leopold unleashed on the Congo were well renumerated for their work, which led to other abuses – famously they received payment for any kill they were sent to carry out and, with no other means of identification, were paid on producing the hand or foot of the victim. This meant that it was often better simply to amputate the limb, and one person could, over time, be the source of several death payments.

Gradually information about what was happening in the Congo began to leak out, and a number of writers took to the cause, including Joseph Conrad, whose novel *Heart of Darkness* (later adapted as the movie *Apocalypse Now*) was set in the Congo, and Arthur Conan Doyle, author of the Sherlock Holmes stories, who wrote *The Crime of the Congo* in response to the atrocities. He said that he was "strongly of the opinion" that the crimes which Leopold was committing in the Congo were "the greatest to be ever known". Mark Twain also wrote about his horror at what was taking place.

In the Congo itself, there were attempts at fighting back, but these rebellions were put down with the same ferocity as marked the rest of Leopold's rule. Meanwhile, he continued to grow rich – richer – through the rubber trade and by the ivory taken from slaughtered elephants. But pressure was growing on other governments to stop what was now being recognized as crimes against humanity.

Finally, in 1908, Leopold was forced to give up his "asset", and the Congo became a colony along the lines of other European colonies – still not allowed self-determination, but some sort of improvement. Leopold covered up his crimes, burning all the records of his time as owner of the Congo, declaring of the other powers, "They have no right to know what I did there."

A year later he died at Laeken in Belgium from an embolism, ending his rule of 44 years. His funeral cortege was booed by the Belgian crowd. The Congo remained under Belgian rule until 1960, when it gained independence, and is now the Democratic Republic of Congo. Demands by the Congo and the United Nations for Belgium to apologize for Leopold's evil acts have been met with resistance by the monarchy – but statues of the tyrant of the Congo have been taken down, and his name lives on mostly in disgrace.

POL POT

They called them "the Killing Fields", and they are the site of what one historian has called "the purest genocide of the Cold War era". Although the carnage in Cambodia lasted only three short years, from 1976 to 1979, ongoing investigations put the death toll at somewhere between 1.7 and 2.2 million, out of a population of 8 million. Examination of gravesites has put the number who were executed by the government at 1.3 million alone, with a million more dead to starvation.

This was all the work of one man whose name would become notorious throughout the world – Pol Pot, the dictator of Cambodia.

He had been born Saloth Sâr to a rich farmer in 1925, when Cambodia was under French control. A poor student, he failed high school and trained as a carpenter, and then he went to Paris to study electronics. It was in Paris that he came under the influence of the French Communist Party and joined other Cambodians in forming the Khmer Rouge (the Red Khmers), the Khmers being the largest ethnic group of Cambodians. When Cambodia became independent in 1953, Pol Pot moved back home – he had failed at university as he had at high school.

For the next 17 years, the Khmer Rouge was part of a revolutionary force which aimed to overthrow the rule of King Norodom Sihanouk. In 1970, when Sihanouk was on holiday in France, a coup took over the government, placing Cambodia under the control of the Soviets, the Chinese and the North Vietnamese Viet Cong. Sihanouk remained as leader, but the country was plunged into civil war, with various factions, including the Khmer Rouge, now led by Pol Pot, fighting for power. By 1976, the Khmer Rouge had taken control of all of Cambodia. Sihanouk was placed under house arrest, and Pol Pot declared a one-party state. He then unleashed pure evil on his people.

The entire population was made to wear black. Money was abolished, and many of the urban population were forced out into the countryside and made to work on collective farms owned by the state. With no money, there were no wages – the workers simply had to obey whatever the Khmer Rouge ordered. Weeks were ten days long, with one day off between. Sport was banned, as was travel. The only reading material permitted was the state newspaper.

It was, like the Congo a hundred years earlier, a slave state.

Those who disobeyed or who were held to be suspect – "bad elements", they were called – were slaughtered, and they were told at their trial, "To keep you is no profit, to destroy you is no loss." The bodies were then taken to the farms and buried – they became fertilizer. This is why the journalist Dith Pran dubbed Cambodia "the Killing Fields", a name also adopted for a monument to the deaths in Phnom Penh.

(Dith himself suffered at the hands of Pol Pot – he had been working for the New York Times, covering the revolution. When the Khmer Rouge imposed its totalitarian state, the

US journalists were allowed to leave Cambodia. Dith spent the next four years in a labour camp, suffering torture and degradation. His story would later become the film *The Killing Fields*.)

Pol Pot also set up security prisons, where perceived enemies of the state could be tortured and killed in what he called "purges". The most notorious was known as S-21 – something like 20,000 people were killed, all of them tortured and forced to confess their crimes before they died, and a crime could be as simple as thinking badly of the state.

In addition, the Khmer Rouge carried out genocide against the ethnic minorities that made up 15 per cent of the population. By the end of the three years, there were barely any survivors.

The violence of the government spread. Cadres of Pol Pot's followers attacked communities and tortured anyone they disliked. One method of death was particularly terrible. In Cambodia, a koan kroach is an amulet containing a mummified foetus – "koan kroach" means "dried child". These amulets were thought to confer strength in battle and were obtained by removing a foetus from the womb of a living woman. The woman is expected to die as the foetus is removed – for the amulet to work it must be an only child. Lost to history, the practice restarted under Pol Pot, and he gave it his blessing.

In 1978, Pol Pot launched his most aggressive purge against anyone believed to be sympathizers with Vietnam – Pol Pot's arch enemy. Tens of thousands of Cambodians were killed in what Pol Pot called an act of purification. These corpses were then added to the killing fields.

But Pol Pot had not reckoned with the strength of the Vietnamese army, which had recently defeated the US. On Christmas Day 1978, Vietnam launched an invasion. The weakened Cambodian population didn't stand a chance, and in a mere 17 days, the capital, Phnom Penh, had fallen. Pol Pot and his fellow leaders fled to Thailand. He would spend the next 20 years trying to regain control of Cambodia, with various levels of success. In 1997, he suffered a stroke, and in 1998, he was arrested in Thailand and charged with crimes against humanity. In an interview he denied all charges, claiming "everything I did, I did for my country". He was sentenced to life imprisonment.

On 15 April 1998, he died. The official cause of death was a heart attack, but it is believed he committed suicide after learning he would be handed over to the US for war crimes. His reign had only lasted three years, and yet Pol Pot's evil will be talked about for centuries.

MUAMMAR GADDAFI

From day one, he later said, he had no doubts about his destiny.

The fourth child of a nomadic Bedouin group in Libya, he was the first son. The tribe kept no written records, so we don't know if he was born in 1942 or 1943. We do know that at the time of his birth, Libya was ruled by Britain and France. But by the time he died, there was only one ruler – the same who had been in power for over 40 years – Muammar Muhammad Abu Minyar al-Gaddafi, known to the world as Colonel Gaddafi.

Unlike the rest of his family, he went to school, his father making great sacrifices to get his son into education. Many of the teachers were Egyptian, and Gaddafi became aware of the independence movement in that country. In 1961, as a late teen, he helped organize demonstrations against the pro-Western monarchy that Europe had installed.

Two years earlier, in 1959, vast oil reserves had been found, and Libya was transformed overnight from a poor country to an incredibly rich one. Then, in 1963, the king, Idris, abolished Libya's ancient feudal system and ordered centralized control over law and taxes. The move was hugely unpopular, and Idris found his position becoming weak. For the next six years, he would cling to power in the face of increasing numbers of protests, which became more and more violent.

Meanwhile, Gaddafi was rising through the armed ranks, having joined the military in 1963. There were rumours he attempted to assassinate his British commander. He also established the revolutionary group, the Central Committee of the Free Officers Movement, named after a similar movement in Egypt. He spent time training in Britain, which he hated, and refused to dress in Western clothes, wearing his Libyan robes around London.

On his return to Libya, he continued to agitate for revolution, and in 1969, a chance arose – Idris went to Turkey for medical treatment, and the Free Officers Movement struck in what they called Operation Jerusalem. The coup took less than 12 hours, and there were no deaths – instead, Gaddafi was hailed as a hero. He was not yet 30, but the boy from a nomadic group was now ruler of the Republic of Libya. His motto was "freedom, socialism and unity".

At first, powers such as Britain and the US worked with Gaddafi, in the hope that they could keep their military bases in Libya. But Gaddafi made them leave. It was his first demonstration of outright hostility to the West, which would see his reign draw him closer and closer to terrorist organizations and countries hostile to Western power, particularly the US.

He was a man of huge ambitions – Libya, a tiny Arab backwater when he was a boy, would become one of the world's great powers. Just as he had started from humble origins, so had his country. He reminded Libyans that when the Prophet Muhammad had called on the Persian and Roman kings to convert to Islam, they had done so. Now he, a Bedouin shepherd, would do the same to the great powers.

He dreamed of unification with Egypt, and in 1973, sent hundreds of his followers across the border, asking Egyptians to sign forms demanding an instant merger. This they were to do in blood. They refused.

He tried other Arab nations with no more success. And so he turned his dreams of an all-powerful state inward, to his own people. He declared Libya the "Great Jamahiriya", meaning the State of the Masses. This was supposed to be a mystical new way of politics; in reality, it was a system of totalitarianism based on a leadership cult. Gaddafi's charisma made it work, but it required severe repression of the general population and the assassination of political enemies.

His vanity was legendary – he would change his outfit several times a day, and he carried a gold revolver encrusted with precious jewels. He had a bodyguard made up entirely of women called the Amazonian Guard, who were sworn to celibacy – but after his death, each of them claimed to have been raped several times by Gaddafi. One woman was kept in a basement for six years and regularly sexually assaulted.

He failed to produce nuclear weapons, but he was able to produce chemical weapons, including mustard gas, which he used in various wars with neighbouring states, including Egypt. But it was his own people who would rise against him.

Inspired by the Arab Spring of 2011, which saw many Arab states overthrow dictators, Libyans rose against the brutality and corruption of Gaddafi's rule. He responded by having his army open fire on protests, killing hundreds. Those who were captured were tortured as Gaddafi vowed to hunt them down "street by street, house by house and wardrobe by wardrobe".

But it was Gaddafi who was the hunted. With the capital taken by protestors, he fled, trying to get back to the area where he was born, but his convoy was stopped. Gaddafi was attacked, stabbed and thrown onto the front of a pick-up truck, falling in front of it as it drove off. He was then thrown in the truck and taken to hospital – but he was dead by the time he got there, having been shot in the stomach.

His body was stored and then put on public display for four days. Thousands came to see it – and to make sure the tyrant was dead.

YAHYA KHAN

The numbers are staggering. Up to 3 million dead. And up to 400,000 women raped. Taken alone these would present one of the most appalling crimes in human history. But what makes it all the more remarkable is that all this carnage happened in less than nine months – that is, over 300,000 deaths a month, and almost 45,000 rapes, nearly 1,500 a day. The Bangladesh Genocide is almost too terrible to contemplate. Its architect was a man known in military circles for his upright morals, preferring to spend time with his family rather than drink with his fellow soldiers – Yahya Khan.

Born in Punjab, which was part of India, in 1917 under British rule, and the son of a policeman, he joined the army in 1939 and fought for the Allies in North Africa, before being taken as a prisoner of war to Italy. He escaped and continued to serve, returning to India at the end of the war.

When India was partitioned and Pakistan created in 1947, Yahya Khan joined the Pakistan Army, and by 1966, he had risen to be its commander-in-chief. By now the country was split into West Pakistan, which is roughly the Pakistan we know today, and East Pakistan, which is roughly what we know as Bangladesh.

Unrest throughout the country in 1969 saw the president, Ayub Khan, seek Yahya Khan's assistance. Yahya Khan imposed martial law on the country, and when Ayub Khan stood down, he became Pakistan's third president. His first statement as president was blunt: "I will not tolerate disorder."

East Pakistan's Bengali majority continued to agitate for change, believing themselves to be discriminated against. Some wanted equal rights, others wanted to secede from Pakistan and become their own nation. Yahya Khan wanted neither. As unrest grew, he decided to act.

On the night of 25 March 1971, the Pakistan Army launched Operation Searchlight. Leading it was the army chief of staff, General Tikka Khan, later dubbed the "Butcher of Bengal" for his role in what followed. The plan was to suppress all opposition in 24 hours, and on that first night, it was estimated around 7,000 Bengalis were killed. A huge number – but later dwarfed by the scale of the bloodbath to come.

The resistance did not end after a day. Yahya Khan's plan to take all the major cities took two months of bloodshed, but even at the end of that, the majority of the countryside remained untamed. Journalists described the atrocities carried out by the army – men were forced to expose themselves to show if they were uncircumcised and therefore Hindu. Those that were Hindu were shot. Women were raped as standard. Entire communities were loaded onto trucks and driven away for "disposal" – usually by being bludgeoned to death to save bullets. President Yahya Khan commanded more reprisals, and General Tikka Khan agreed.

Cities such as Dhaka were razed to the ground and bulldozed until they barely existed. Those who were there when the killings began and took shelter found the buildings they hid in set alight. Notable intellectuals were hunted down and sentenced to death on the spot.

The soldiers were also actively encouraged to rape Hindu women – this was regarded as "war booty". Gang rapes were common, as women who had watched their husbands and children die were used by lines of men. Military brothels were established with women held captive and used.

One journalist found a brothel with 563 captives, some as young as eight, some as old as 75. These rape camps would play a part in producing a generation of war babies – somewhere between 25,000 and 70,000 children were born to victims in the camps, while there were an estimated 170,000 terminations performed. After the conflict many of these women and children lived lives of shame. Pakistan's government has remained silent.

Yahya Khan's brutality led to a flood of refugees from East Pakistan into India, and in December 1971, India was forced to react. Within 13 days, they had forced Pakistan to surrender and Yahya Khan to resign – he was immediately placed under house arrest. General Tikka Khan, however, was promoted to commander-in-chief of the whole Pakistan army. East Pakistan became an independent country known as Bangladesh.

Yahya Khan remained under house arrest until 1979 and died in 1980 after a life of heavy drinking. He is widely hated in Pakistan for a war that broke the country in half. But he is also hated throughout the world for the Bangladesh genocide, which remains one of humanity's worst crimes.

PAPA DOC

The year – 1967. The president of Haiti strode to the microphone to give a public address. A few days earlier bombs had been detonated near the Presidential Palace, and members of the military were held to be responsible. So before he spoke, he did a roll call of officers who were in attendance, having each one call "Present". Nineteen didn't respond, and he said "Absent" for them. The list completed, the president leaned into the microphone and said of those who were absent, "All were shot." Welcome to the world of François Duvalier, known to the world as Papa Doc.

The ruler of Haiti from 1957 until his death in 1971, his was one of the most repressive regimes in the Western Hemisphere. Estimates vary on how many of his political enemies he killed, but it is thought to be about 60,000. So 19 officers shot on suspicion of treason was small beer to Papa Doc.

Communism was outlawed – the punishment for any such suspicious behaviour was instant death, no trial. The old elite was eliminated, mostly by force, to be replaced with his corrupt new elite. Peasant landholdings were confiscated and given to his military supporters, whose ineptitude led to mass starvation. Staggering numbers died from an entirely man-made famine.

He had been born in 1907, the son of a justice of the peace and a baker. For most of his adult life he was a physician – hence his nickname, bestowed on him by his patients. But as well as his medical work, he started to become involved in Black nationalism, founding a journal arguing for the elimination of the US occupation of Haiti, which had begun in 1915.

He also grew interested in Haitian voodoo, with its devotion to spells and occult powers – he would use this knowledge throughout his presidency to give him a veneer of greater powers than just those of the gun. Around this time, he also married Simone Ovide, with whom he had four children.

In 1946, he aligned with the new president, Dumarsais Estimé, but he was forced to go into hiding after a coup by Colonel Paul Magloire. The Magloire presidency was a fragile one, and Papa Doc announced his candidacy. When Magloire fled Haiti in 1957, Papa Doc and wealthy sugar planter Louis Déjoie fought an election. Papa Doc won the election with 72.4 per cent of the vote. At the age of 50, he was president of Haiti.

The first thing he did was exile Déjoie's supporters. This showed more restraint than he would become known for. He also dismissed all high-ranking officials, including those in the army, who did not pledge absolute loyalty to him. He also created his own rural militia, called the Tontons Macoutes, which means bogeymen, who could carry out his orders and act as a secret police force. It quickly spread fear among much of the rural population. The bogeymen had free rein to do whatever they wanted and would often tie victims to chairs, then slit their throats and leave them in public or hang them in the marketplace as a warning to others.

Then, on 24 May 1959, Papa Doc suffered a heart attack, which left him, according to physicians, with some neurological damage. Was this part of the reason that the strict leader became an absolute autocrat? Certainly, the man who patients revered for his care as a doctor became more ruthless and more bloodthirsty after this time.

For example, when a voodoo doctor told him that a political opponent, Clément Barbot, had turned into a black dog, Papa Doc had every black dog in Haiti exterminated. He also ordered that peepholes be placed in all interrogation chambers so he could watch opponents and criminals being tortured to death, sometimes by being placed in sulphuric acid. The head of another opponent, Blucher Philogenes, was removed, and Papa Doc kept it in his closet.

By the terms of the Haitian constitution, 1963 should have seen the end of his presidency – all presidencies were to be for one six-year term. But this former champion of freedom held a referendum to ask if he should be re-elected. The result was 1,320,748 "yes" votes and 0 "no" votes – it was obviously rigged. A second referendum granted him the position of President for Life, this time with 99.9% in favour, 0.01% against. Who the 0.01% was is a mystery, as the ballot papers were all marked with Yes in advance.

In addition to his military control of the population, Papa Doc also assumed spiritual control. He declared himself not only as one with the voodoo spirits, the "Iwa", but with Jesus Christ and even God. Jesus had, he claimed, chosen him to lead Haiti, perhaps the world. His official title became "Incorruptible Leader of the Great Majority of the Haitian People, Renovator of the Republic, Chief of the Revolution and Spiritual Father of the Nation".

These claims appeared on huge posters that adorned the capital city, Port-au-Prince, and Papa Doc would often order rallies of peasants, who were trucked into the city to chant his name. In school, children were ordered to pray to him.

But if they prayed for him, it didn't work. In 1971, at the age of 64, he died of heart disease. When he died, 90 per cent of the population was illiterate, a dramatic increase in his time in power, and the average wage was US$75 a year, compared with $400 in the rest of Latin America.

Due to other changes in the constitution, his 19-year-old son Jean-Claude, known as Baby Doc, took over the presidency. When Baby Doc himself was deposed in a 1986 coup sponsored by the US, protestors attacked Duvalier's mausoleum, throwing boulders at it, chipping off pieces from it and breaking open the crypt. But the body of the dictator was gone. A final act of voodoo?

SERIAL
KILLERS AND
PSYCHOPATHS

As much as tyrants and dictators can terrify us, there is something about the intimacy of the serial killer which provokes true feelings of horror. These are men who the victims saw up close at the hour of their deaths. Often, the victim spent their final moments in pain and fear, alone in the world, reduced to a body to be hurt and then terminated.

And what of the eyes of the killer? To be killed like this is to confront another human who knows no mercy, who knows no morality, who wants only one thing at that moment. Can one reason with a serial killer? Can one appeal to their better nature? Maybe earlier, maybe later, but at that moment when the desire to kill takes over, no serial killer can be turned back from their mission.

And yet, they fascinate us as much as they repel us. What is this animal part of the human that will allow it to carry out such barbaric acts? How can we tame it? Worse, what is this part of being human that makes it an even more ruthless, even more inventive killer than other members of the animal kingdom? A cat's instincts may lead it to play with its prey before killing it, but what makes a man plan, consider and then carry out the murder of another human being? Is it from the desire to cause suffering?

TED BUNDY

When people think of serial killers, one name always occurs at the head of the list – it has almost become synonymous with the term "serial killer". The name "Ted Bundy" has haunted the human imagination for years, inspiring fear and disgust. He killed his victims, he decapitated them, he had sex with their corpses. It is hard to think of anyone who has plumbed such depths of human depravity. He is known to have killed 30 women, but some estimates put the true total at closer to 100.

Chillingly, it was his charm and intelligence that most people who met him remembered and which helped him carry out his crimes. His chosen victims were invariably similar – attractive college women. Wearing his arm in a sling or walking with the aid of crutches, he would ask for assistance carrying things. Or he would impersonate a police officer or firefighter. Anything he could do to get his potential victims in his tan 1968 Volkswagen. And then the horror began.

He was born in 1946 and was immediately recognized as intelligent and shy. Well-liked at school, he went to college at the University of Washington, studying Chinese and then psychology, and being active in student politics. With his charm and charisma, it was thought he may one day run for office. What his fellow students didn't know was that he had already become addicted to pornography and would often spend his nights watching women through windows and masturbating.

But fantasies were not enough. He wanted to act on them. On 4 January 1974, aged 28, he did.

Her name was Karen Sparks, and she was 18 years old. She was alone in her Washington basement flat at 1 a.m. when she thought she saw a man looking through the window. He was there for only a moment, and she thought she may have imagined it. Then she went to sleep.

She had not imagined it. There was a man – Ted Bundy. He had broken into her room as she slept. He tore a part of the bedframe off her bed and used it to bludgeon her. He then used one of the poles to sexually assault her, splitting her bladder. She lay there bleeding for 20 hours after the assault before one of her returning housemates found her. She survived the attack. Only one other of Bundy's victims would do so.

We are not sure what happened to 21-year-old Lynda Ann Healy, a fellow psychology student at Washington. We only know she was snatched from her bed on 1 February 1974 and that Bundy would later claim her as his first kill. Her skull was discovered a year later, with the remains of four other women.

Bundy had now crossed the line into murder. For the next few months, women went missing at the rate of about one a month, all of them Washington students. No bodies were found, and nothing connected the disappearances to the assault on Karen Sparks. There had been some sightings of a man on crutches near where the women were last seen, but there was no solid evidence.

The disappearances then shifted from Washington to Oregon, 350 miles away. The MO was the same, as were the profiles of the victims. A man on crutches had been seen, or sometimes one with his arm in a sling. Crucially, a tan 1968 Volkswagen had also been seen in the area, as it had in Washington.

The police checked it out and found the vehicle belonged to a college student called Ted Bundy. But investigations revealed him to be a bright and charming young man. No further action was taken.

He then moved to Utah, and women began to go missing there and in nearby Colorado. Some reports started to come in from women who had been approached by a man with his arm in a sling, but they had not gone with him. Same charming manner. Same Volkswagen.

What they did not know is that the women who did get in the car were not just the victims of sexual assault and murder. Bundy also used their corpses for macabre sexual pleasure. He spent a long time with the dead bodies before disposing of them, often keeping them laying down in the passenger seat of the Volkswagen while he used them.

It was a simple error which finally stopped the spree on 16 August 1975. Seeing a police car approach – he did not know they weren't looking for him – Bundy sped off in the Volkswagen, and a car chase ensued. When the police caught him, they found in his car a ski mask, a second mask fashioned from tights, a crowbar, handcuffs, rubbish bags, a coil of rope and an ice pick. They also discovered female hair, which would be found to match that of some of his victims.

He was arrested for kidnap while the police built up evidence. He was sentenced to 15 years and then stood trial for murder.

Somehow, he escaped.

He had used his charm to be allowed to use the prison library to study for his own defence. Not having to wear shackles, he leaped from a second-storey window and ran away. He was picked up six days later and placed in prison in Glenwood Springs, Colorado. He again escaped, using a makeshift hacksaw to cut a hole in his cell wall.

He fled to Florida, where he kept a low profile until January 1978, when his psychopathic tendencies returned. Breaking into Florida State University one night, he attacked and raped four women in 15 minutes, leaving two dead. He bit the buttocks of one of the killed women, Lisa Levy, and these bitemarks would be a key part of his trial. An hour later he raped another woman before fleeing.

He drove 150 miles to Jacksonville and approached a 14-year-old, but he fled again when her older brother confronted him. His final victim was 12-year-old Kimberly Dianne Leach, whom he raped and killed on 8 February 1978. By now the evil that consumed him knew no boundaries.

When he was finally arrested on 12 February 1978, he told the police that he wished they had killed him. It would be another 11 years before he was finally executed, on 24 January 1989. Having initially protested his innocence, he confessed in order to try and delay the execution by offering up information about where he had buried bodies – negotiating over the bodies of the women he had raped, killed and committed necrophilia with was his final evil act.

JEFFREY DAHMER

There is a fine line, they say, between what makes us human and what makes us an animal. In the case of someone like Jeffrey Dahmer, that line is virtually invisible. Over the course of 13 years, he killed at least 17 men. But he did so much more once they were dead. He dismembered them. He had sex with their corpses. And he crossed one of the most terrifying lines of all – he became a cannibal and feasted on their dead flesh. And the dead flesh he didn't feast on he kept and continued to use for sexual gratification, even once it was rotted and covered in maggots.

He was born in Milwaukee, Wisconsin in 1960, and some disturbing signs were there early. His mother suffered from depression and attempted suicide at least once. Dahmer was fascinated by dead animals as a child and asked his father, a research chemist, about how they were put together and how they could be preserved. By the time he was a teenager, he had started to dissect them, including a dog which he killed and then cut to pieces, nailing the parts to a tree.

But animals weren't enough.

On 18 June 1978, three weeks after he graduated from high school and now living with his grandmother, Dahmer picked up a hitchhiker, 18-year-old Steven Mark Hicks. He invited Hicks home, and they drank beer together. Dahmer was hoping they would have sex, but it soon became clear Hicks was into girls. When Hicks attempted to leave, Dahmer beat him with a dumbbell. He then used the dumbbell to strangle Hicks and masturbated on the corpse.

He was not finished with Hicks yet, however. He dragged the body down to the basement, dismembered it, and continued to use it for sexual pleasure. He buried the pieces in the backyard, but still the evil inside him would not rest. A few weeks later he dug the pieces up, cut away the flesh, dissolved it in acid and crushed the bones. He then flushed it all away in the toilet.

Perhaps he was shocked by what he had done, because it was nine years before he killed again, although during that time, he received a year's probation for masturbating in front of two 12-year-olds, and he had once tried to dig up a corpse from a graveyard. But he gave up when the ground was too hard.

But on 20 November 1987, it seems it all got too much. The victim was 25-year-old Steven Tuomi, and Dahmer lured him back to a hotel. His plan had been to drug Tuomi and use him while he was unconscious. But he woke in the morning to find Tuomi dead – his chest was caved in, he was bleeding from the mouth, and Dahmer's arms were covered in bruises. He would later say he had no memory of what had happened.

Panicked, he bought a large suitcase and took Tuomi's body back to his grandmother's house. There he dismembered it, disposing of it all except the head, which he kept for sexual pleasure. When the flesh started to rot, he boiled it off. He retained the skull to keep using it. When it became too fragile, he disposed of it too.

By now he could not hold back. James Doxtator, a 14-year-old Native American prostitute, and 22-year-old Richard Guerrero, who Dahmer met in a bar, were his next victims, and again he kept their bodies and used them for sexual pleasure. They were stored in the basement of his grandmother's house until the overwhelming smell made her ask him to leave, although she did not investigate further.

Over the course of 1990, Dahmer killed four men, and in 1991, another eight, including six in a two-month killing spree. His appetites became ever darker, his behaviour more and more horrifying. When he killed 22-year-old Ernest Miller, he took Polaroids of himself with the corpse, and he kissed and talked to the severed head as he dismembered the body. He placed the head of 28-year-old Edward Smith in an oven to dry and it exploded. This was the only time Dahmer expressed any regrets regarding his killing spree – he had lost, he told police, a skull he could have used.

He stored more and more body parts in either his refrigerator or a 57-gallon drum and took photographs of every stage of his murders, from the first pick up through to the final disposal of the bodies. By now he was also feasting on flesh, gaining sexual gratification through having parts of his victims inside him.

Of the 1991 killings, he regarded the death of 23-year-old Jeremiah Weinberger, his fifteenth victim, as exceptional. Dahmer drilled through Weinberger's skull and injected boiling water and acid into the frontal lobes of his brain in an attempt to make a "sex zombie". Weinberger, Dahmer said, died with his eyes open – a particular thrill.

It was on 22 July 1991 that Dahmer's luck finally ran out. He had lured 32-year-old Tracy Edwards back to his apartment and handcuffed him. Dahmer then pressed a knife to Edwards' chest and said he was going to eat the other man's heart. Edwards, who had only sipped the drugged drink he had been given, managed to punch Dahmer, escape and find police officers. Returning to the apartment, the officers found Dahmer, a large knife and drawers full of Polaroids. Dahmer attempted to resist arrest, but he was pinned to the floor. He told them that for what he had done, he should be dead.

In police interviews, Dahmer described each killing in graphic detail, appearing aroused as he did so. He had planned, he said, to build an altar out of all the skulls he had collected, which he could sit besides, meditate and feel at home.

He was sentenced to 999 years in jail but served only two, being beaten to death by a fellow inmate, Christopher Scarver. Even other murderers found Dahmer too much to stomach.

JACK
THE RIPPER

It is unlikely we will ever know his true identity, but the name the newspapers gave him is still enough to send shivers down any spine. In a time before humanity knew much about serial killers, he terrorized London by carrying out a series of murders, the brutality of which has seldom been surpassed. He is Jack the Ripper, and time has not erased the horror of his acts.

Without biographical details, we are left with his murders alone to try and piece together his methods and his motivation.

What we do know is that from 1888 to 1891, 11 women were murdered in the Whitechapel area of London and that five of them – known as the "canonical five" – seemed definitively to have been killed by the same hand. And these were no ordinary murders. While the East End of London was famed for its violence, nothing had prepared the public for what Jack did.

The murdered women, mostly prostitutes, all died the same way – they had slash wounds to their throats and genitals, their internal organs had been removed and their faces disfigured.

The canonical five were all murdered between 31 August and 9 November 1888.

A few months earlier two women, Emma Elizabeth Smith and Martha Tabram, had been killed after receiving horrific injuries, including to their genitals. In the case of Smith, it appears a gang had attacked her, while Tabram's injuries did not match those of later victims.

It was at 3.40 a.m. on 31 August 1888 that the body of Mary Ann Nichols, known as Polly, was found in Buck's Row, Whitechapel, lying under tarpaulin. Many experts believe this is when the Ripper committed his first gruesome act. Nichols' throat had been stabbed twice down to the vertebrae, her vagina stabbed, and her stomach cut open, revealing her bowels. An autopsy revealed something shocking – the killer seemed to display anatomical precision. Very little blood had been lost, suggesting he was particularly skilled with a knife.

A week later Annie Chapman was found with the same wounds, but they were more extensive. Her stomach had been opened and her small intestine placed beside her. Her uterus and sections of her bladder and vagina had been removed. Again, this was skilled work.

On 30 September, Elizabeth Stride and Catherine Eddowes were both killed. Stride had a single cut across the throat and no other wounds. This suggested that the Ripper was interrupted during the murder, as does the fact that he killed again that night. Eddowes was found 45 minutes later stabbed in the throat, stomach opened, organs removed, the same as the first two deaths.

By now London was in a panic. The brutality of the deaths shocked even the most hardened members of society. Panic was spreading, and it only got worse on 9 November when Mary Jane Kelly was found on her bed with her throat stabbed down to the vertebrae, her stomach opened and the organs removed. Her heart was missing, and her uterus, kidneys and one breast had been placed beneath her head. It seems the Ripper was becoming even more brutal.

Police raided homes and questioned butchers and slaughterers, even surgeons. They received hundreds of letters from people saying they had evidence, many of them claiming to be the murderer. One, which seemed to recount details not revealed to the public, was signed "Jack the Ripper". The newspapers had their name for the suspected killer.

Four other deaths soon followed, but it was impossible to tell if they were by the same killer or a copycat – evil begets evil. But the murders didn't seem to exhibit the same surgical skill as the previous five. Whether Rose Mylett, Alice McKenzie, the Pinchin Street torso and Frances Coles were victims of the Ripper, we will never know. In the case of the torso, found beneath a railway arch on 10 September 1889, we will never even know who she was.

Experts believe that the Ripper's murder spree stopped with Mary Jane Kelly. Perhaps he himself was killed or was incarcerated for another crime, or maybe he just died or moved away. Or perhaps his bloodlust had been fulfilled. Or perhaps he had horrified himself – the last killing had been so extreme that it may have woken him to the terrible evil he had unleashed.

We will never know, but for a few months he held one of the largest cities in the world in his hand, just like he had held his knife.

JOSEF MENGELE

He was known as the Angel of Death. In the horror of the Nazi concentration camps, it is hard to go past the extermination of 6 million Jews when it comes to human depravity. But one man's acts in those camps are horrifying even by those standards. His name was Josef Mengele, and he will go down as one of the most notorious figures in the Nazi Party.

Many have tried to paint Mengele as a mad scientist carrying out sadistic experiments on the prisoners of Auschwitz for no real scientific reasons. The truth is, if anything, more horrifying. Josef Mengele was a respected and highly trained medical professional at the top of his field before the war began. He would use this training in appalling ways, and the suffering he would cause is almost unimaginable.

Born to a Catholic family in 1911, he studied medicine and anthropology. He received his PhD in 1936 and became a fully qualified doctor in 1937. He started work at the ominously titled Institute for Hereditary Biology and Racial Hygiene in Frankfurt and made twins his main research topic, with a particular interest in what caused cleft palates.

But he was also politically active – he had joined a far-right group in 1931 and became a fully-fledged member of the Nazi Party in 1937. This aligned with his embrace of what was known as "racial science" – a fundamental tenet of National Socialism. According to racial science, some races were more evolved and superior to others, and, along with Hitler, he came to believe that the German race was at the top of the evolutionary tree.

Racial science also argued that there should be no mixing of the races. It advocated forced sterilization for inferior races, among which the Nazis included Jews, Black people, Romanis and anyone with a physical "deformity". In his work on twins, Mengele investigated whether subjects claiming to be of German descent were racially and physically suitable to qualify as Germans.

He spent the first few years of the Second World War fighting on the front lines and working as a medical officer, earning the Iron Cross, both 2nd and 1st Class, and promotion to SS captain. Then, in 1943, he was assigned to work in Auschwitz-Birkenau, Germany's most notorious prison camp. More than 1.3 million captives would pass through Auschwitz, and, staggeringly, 1.1 million of those who did were murdered.

Mengele was initially in charge of Romani prisoners in what was disparagingly called "the Gypsy Camp". He participated in selecting the 2,893 Romani prisoners who were to be murdered in the Birkenau gas chambers.

He was moved to the Jewish section, where one of his duties was to decide which prisoners were unfit for hard labour – pregnant women, the elderly, children and those too sick to work. His visits to the camp hospital terrorized the prisoners, as he carried out an examination and decided whether to condemn that prisoner to the gas chamber.

In fact, there were 50 doctors carrying out this process. What made Mengele best known was that he would always be present on the ramp to the gas chamber where selections took place. He was not only selecting those who should die, he was also looking for what he regarded as interesting specimens to experiment on.

His main interest remained twins, and in Auschwitz, where there was no consideration for the victims' health or physical and emotional suffering, he could carry out experiments impossible somewhere else. He would experiment on one twin and use the other as a "control" subject and could therefore compare what happened. He would do things like perform amputations on one twin, give them a disease such as typhus, inject chemicals into their eyes, or remove teeth, hair or organs.

He also experimented on pregnant women, removing children from wombs, deliberately infecting the mother, baby or both. Young children were also useful for his experiments, and he was known for his practice of giving them sweets before experimenting on them and usually killing them. With his belief that Jews were an inferior race, he had no qualms about the suffering he caused.

He also experimented with mass sterilization and performed unnecessary surgery, often without anaesthetics. He selected individuals to be murdered and then dissected in the hope of finding racial markers that could make identification of racial purity easier.

When Auschwitz fell in January 1945, Mengele fled and rejoined the army. Captured by US forces, he became a prisoner of war. But the US failed to identify him as one of the world's most wanted war criminals and released him in August 1945.

After four years working anonymously as a farmhand, he fled Germany for Argentina in 1949. He would spend the next 30 years being chased by West German authorities and Israeli intelligence services from Argentina to Paraguay and Paraguay to Brazil. There, in 1979, he died, suffering a stroke and drowning while swimming at a vacation resort. It was not until six years later that he was traced, his body exhumed and his remains positively identified using DNA testing.

In a final twist, his skeleton is stored at the São Paulo Institute for Forensic Medicine, where it is used as an educational aid during forensic medicine courses. He has the good fortune to have these experiments carried out on him when he can't suffer, unlike those he experimented on himself.

TIMOTHY McVEIGH AND TERRY NICHOLS

At 9.01 on the morning of 19 April 1995, former soldier Timothy McVeigh pulled a rented truck up to the doors of the Alfred P. Murrah Federal Building in Oklahoma City. He parked, got out and walked away. One minute earlier he had lit a two-minute fuse attached to a bomb that he and Terry Nichols had made from agricultural fertilizer, diesel fuel and other chemicals.

At 9.02 a.m., the bomb went off. Some 168 people died, 17 of them children, and another 680 were injured. Another 300 buildings were damaged. It was the largest act of domestic terrorism in the history of the US. As 665 rescue workers rushed to attend the scene, first reports linked the attack to international terrorists taking revenge on the US. But a mere 90 minutes later McVeigh was pulled over for driving his 1977 Mercury Marquis without a licence plate. A concealed weapon in the car led to his arrest, and a card was found which read, "TNT at $5 a stick. Need more."

Federal police had also interviewed the owner of the place the truck had been hired from and produced an identikit picture, which matched McVeigh. By 21 April, McVeigh had been charged with the bombing, and his accomplice, Terry Nichols, had turned himself in. This was no international terrorist incident. To the horror of many Americans, the terrorists were homegrown.

Born in New York in 1968, McVeigh claimed to have been bullied as a child, and he dreamed of revenge against bullies. He would later describe the US government as the world's biggest bully. He won an ironic award at school for "most talkative" – he was almost always silent. At 20, he joined the US Army and served in Iraq. He received one reprimand for purchasing a White Power T-shirt.

In the army, his platoon guide was Terry Nichols. Nichols was from Michigan and had spent his life doing part-time jobs, carpentry work, managing a grain elevator, and selling life insurance and real estate. A bright boy at school and good at art, he had ambitions of becoming a doctor but had fallen short.

He spent one year in the army, slightly less than McVeigh. He told fellow soldiers that one day he would have his own army.

He and McVeigh formed an immediate bond, both being interested in survivalism and both known for their derogatory remarks about Black soldiers. After their service they remained close and grew increasingly paranoid about the federal government. McVeigh at one time claimed the army had implanted a microchip in his backside to track him. And, in 1992, Nichols attempted to renounce his citizenship, declaring himself a "non-resident alien".

Two years earlier a disturbing incident had occurred – in 1990, 35-year-old Nichols had arranged to marry a mail-order bride from the Philippines, 17-year-old Marife Torres. When she arrived, she was pregnant with another man's child. When the child was two, it suffocated on a plastic bag. Both McVeigh and Nichols were suspected of killing the child, but no firm evidence could be found.

The 51-day siege at Waco – where federal officers surrounded the compound of cult leader David Koresh and his Branch Davidians, eventually storming the compound and killing 76 cult members – further enraged them against the government. McVeigh drove to Waco during the siege and handed out pro-gun material. On his return, the pair began to plot their revenge.

On 22 September 1994, they rented a storage shed and began to purchase explosives to store there, including dynamite, diesel fuel and 50 bags of ammonium nitrate fertilizer, enough to fertilize 12.5 acres (5.1 hectares) of farmland. The bomb they built was in 13 barrels, each weighing nearly 230 kg.

They chose the Alfred P. Murrah Federal Building in Oklahoma City because it contained 14 federal agencies and was named after a judge, another target of hatred. McVeigh later said he believed that the windows covering the front would shatter into the carpark and non-federal people would be protected from harder material shooting outwards. In fact, the breaking glass accounted for 5 per cent of the deaths.

The plan was to attack at 11 a.m., but McVeigh could not wait. He wore a printed T-shirt with *Sic semper tyrannis* ("Thus always to tyrants"), and he carried a copy of a white supremacist book and an envelope full of anti-government propaganda. He pulled up, lit the fuse and fled, deliberately dropping the keys to the truck as he jumped into his getaway car, its licence plates removed.

Two hours later he was behind bars, as he would be for the rest of his life. On 11 June 2001, McVeigh was executed by lethal injection. He gave no final statement.

Terry Nichols was sentenced to the longest jail sentence in US history, 161 consecutive life terms without the possibility of parole. The judge said, "No American citizen has ever brought this kind of devastation; you are the No. 1 mass murderer in all of US history."

They had performed only one evil act, but their names would go down in infamy.

ALBERT FISH

Dapper isn't a word most associated with serial killers. And yet in his mugshot, taken in 1903, Albert Fish does look dapper. His moustache is waxed, his collar high and his bowler hat is straight as a die. The sort of man a society woman at the beginning of the twentieth century might have taken home to meet her parents.

But she would have made a terrible mistake.

An X-ray taken at the same time as his mugshot revealed that as well as a tiepin, Fish also had 29 needles lodged in his pelvis, which he had forced there himself for self-gratification. He was also known to use a nail-studded paddle to beat his own buttocks and to push petrol-soaked cotton wool inside his anus and set it alight.

But self-harm was the least of the horrors. The dapper Albert Fish was a serial killer, rapist, child molester and cannibal who claimed to have 100 victims and that he had produced a child in every State of the US.

He was born in Washington, D.C. in 1870 to a father 43 years older than his mother. There was a history of mental illness in his immediate family, including two of his brothers and his sister. He was just five when his 75-year-old father died, and he was placed in an orphanage, where he suffered regular beatings. Over time he found sexual pleasure in these, and when he left the orphanage, he became involved with a telegraph boy, the pair drinking their own urine and eating each other's faeces.

In his twenties, he moved to New York, where he became a male prostitute and began molesting young boys. Despite his inclinations, he married at 28 and had six legitimate children, some of whom he forced to use the nail-studded paddle on him. The 1903 mugshot was taken when he was arrested for grand larceny, but he also spent time in mental institutions around the same period.

On release his tastes became ever more perverse – once, aged 40, he saw a bisected penis in a wax museum and desired to see the same in real life. He started up a relationship with an intellectually disabled 19-year-old, Thomas Keddon. One day, he took Keddon to "an old farmhouse" – and then tortured him for two weeks. Finally, he cut off Keddon's penis. He later said he never forgot the scream or the look Keddon gave him. Wrapping the amputated penis in a handkerchief and leaving a $10 note, Fish said he took the first train he could get back home. He never heard what became of Keddon.

He started hearing the voice of God, and it told him he should not only kill children but that he should sexually assault and torture them first. He paid other boys to procure victims, then used what he called "implements of Hell" on them: meat cleavers, saws and butcher's knives. Most of his victims were mentally disabled – he thought there was less chance of them being missed, and we certainly have no records of how many he killed, nor was he counting.

It was in 1928, at the age of 58, that Fish committed the crime that finally saw him captured. He saw a classified ad that read, "Young man, 18, wishes position in country. Edward Budd, 406 West 15th Street." Fish visited on the pretence of hiring the young man, intending to sexually assault, torture and kill him.

But his interest immediately fell on Edward Budd's younger sister, Grace, aged ten. He convinced her parents to let her come to his "niece's birthday party". The parents allowed him. He took Grace to an abandoned house, murdered her and ate her. He then wrote to her parents describing what he had done to her in great detail – his meal had lasted nine days, he told them.

He had made one crucial error – the envelope he had placed the letter in was embossed with the initials NYPCBA – the New York Private Chauffeur's Benevolent Association. The janitor at the association had taken some of these envelopes back to the rooming house where he and Fish were staying. Fish had taken one. The police descended at last on Albert Fish.

They could not in their most terrible dreams have imagined the crimes that Fish would spend the next days and weeks confessing to. At first, they thought he must be lying, but as matches were found for some of the missing children, the horrible truth dawned on them – Albert Fish was no fantasist, these were his actual crimes, and they included murder, rape, paedophilia and cannibalism. Two other children were also his victims, but the toll of the man now dubbed the Brooklyn Vampire was definitely much higher.

He was charged only with the murder of Grace Budd, but it was more than enough to guarantee the death sentence. Fish's lawyer, attempting to prove his client was insane, detailed Fish's sexual perversions, including sadism and masochism, flagellation, exhibitionism, voyeurism, cannibalism, coprophagia, urophilia, paedophilia, necrophilia and infibulation.

The judge and jury rejected the insanity plea – or at least, as one juror said, even though he was insane, they believed he should be killed. At 11.06 p.m. on 16 January 1936, Fish was placed in the electric chair. His final words were allegedly that he didn't know why he was there. His defence counsel never released Fish's final statement, written a few hours before his death, saying, "I will never show it to anyone. It was the most filthy string of obscenities that I have ever read."

There is a photograph of Fish being strapped into the electric chair. As in the mugshot, he stares straight at the camera. That stare would have been the last thing many poor unfortunates saw.

IVAN MILAT

The Australian bush has always held a fascination – a place of mystery where strange things can happen. To enter the bush can be to leave the comforts of humanity and encounter nature in its most primal form. And sometimes you do so in a place so remote that no one can hear you scream.

For the most part, the Belanglo State Forest in New South Wales has not carried any of these sinister overtones, being a popular destination for campers and backpackers. A place to take the family and get away from it all, but not too far away.

All of that changed in late 1989. On 29 December, a pair of backpackers, Deborah Everist, 19, and James Gibson, 19, from Victoria in southern Australia, were reported missing in the forest. Both were experienced backpackers, and it seemed very odd that they would have got lost. But no bodies were found.

Then, in January 1991, Simone Schmidl, 21, from Germany, also went missing. On Boxing Day that same year, two other Germans, Gabor Neugebauer, 21, and Anja Habschied, 20, disappeared. And finally, two British backpackers, Caroline Clarke, 21, and Joanne Walters, 22, disappeared on 18 April 1992.

It seemed more than odd that so many backpackers between the ages of 19 and 22 would go missing in such a short space of time in a similar area, especially as many of them were travelling in pairs. Police – and the public – could see only one explanation. There was a serial killer working in the forest.

Suspicions were confirmed in September 1992. The bodies of the two British backpackers, Caroline Clarke and Joanne Walters, were discovered. Clarke had been shot ten times in the head at the burial site, and the police believe she had been used as target practice. Walters had been stabbed 14 times: four times in the chest, once in the neck and nine times in the back, which would have paralyzed her before she died.

Panic spread. Belanglo became a no-go area, as people were terrified of suffering the same ordeal. This only intensified a year later when the bodies of Deborah Everist and James Gibson were found. Gibson had been stabbed eight times, and again would have been paralyzed by a knife in the spine. Everist's jaw was broken, her skull fractured and she too had been stabbed in the spine. Autopsy reports showed that most of the victims had not died instantly. They had been paralyzed and then tortured.

This was no ordinary killer. It was a psychopath who obviously enjoyed tormenting their victims.

Less than a month later the body of Simone Schmidl was found as part of the search, again stabbed, again including the spine. And three days later the other two Germans, Habschied and Neugebauer, were found. Habschied had been decapitated, and Neugebauer shot in the head six times.

The story became an international sensation due to the nationalities of the victims and the brutality of the crimes. When one man in England heard the news, a chill went down his spine. Paul Onions had spent three years struggling to sleep and developing a string of illnesses which would later be put down to shock.

He had also been backpacking in Belanglo, back in 1990. He was hitchhiking when he was picked up by a man named "Bill", who said he was from a Yugoslav family and worked on the roads. As they drove, Bill's behaviour became stranger and stranger, constantly varying his speed and looking in the rearview mirror. When Bill pulled over and got out of the car, Onions did too. Bill ordered him to get back in the car. He obeyed, and then Bill pulled out a revolver, telling Onions this was a robbery. Onions managed to leap from the car and run.

When he heard the news story, he contacted New South Wales police. One of their suspects was indeed a Yugoslav man who worked on the roads. His name was Ivan Milat, and the moment Onions saw him he knew it was the same man.

The fifth of 14 children to an alcoholic Croatian father and Australian mother, Milat had a long history of violence. As a child he attacked animals with machetes, and by 17, he was in juvenile detention for theft. He reoffended on release, and at 22, he was serving three years in prison. In 1971, aged 26, he abducted two female hitchhikers, raping one before they escaped. He was again arrested but fled, and later he found work for the New South Wales government's road department. He would often boast about his capacity for violence.

On 22 May 1994, 50 police descended on Milat's house, and there they found a huge cache of weapons, many of which matched those used in the attacks. Despite the overwhelming evidence, Milat pleaded not guilty. His trial lasted 18 weeks, and the prosecution called on 145 witnesses. On 27 July 1996, Milat was found guilty of seven murders and sentenced to seven life sentences.

His depravity continued in prison – he once cut one of his own fingers off with a plastic knife with the intention of mailing it to the High Court of Australia to force an appeal. He also carried out a nine-day hunger strike in the hope of getting a PlayStation.

Throughout, he continued to deny that he had committed the crimes and refused every attempt to tell police where the other bodies were. He was also a "person of interest" in a number of other cases of robbery, disappearances and what appeared to be murders. But he told police nothing which could have helped with their enquiries or brought comfort to any of the victims' families.

He died of cancer in 2019, aged 74.

DAVID BERKOWITZ

It was hot. Famously so. The heatwave that gripped New York in 1976 left a city of 16 million people on edge. There were, it was estimated, something like 1,000 homicides in New York that year, and the police just couldn't keep up. Some of the murders were gangland slayings. Some were during robberies. Some were domestic. But some seemed to occur just to release the pressure in a place at boiling point.

Six of those killings stood out for their brutality and their darkness – and for the way the killer taunted the police and the public. They were, it was soon realized, the work of a single killer, who the papers dubbed the Son of Sam. In fact, ask a true New Yorker about 1976, and they will still call it not the Summer of Disco but the Summer of Sam.

We know now, but no one knew then, that his name was David Berkowitz. Given up for adoption as a child, he had grown up in the Bronx. He briefly served with the US Army in South Korea and had struggled to hold down a job. In 1976, he was working as a letter sorter for the United States Postal Service.

He had met his birth mother one year earlier and been told about the way he had been given up for adoption as an unwanted child. He found the question of his identity disturbing and started to carry out petty crimes, and he soon stabbed a woman with a knife. He then got himself a .44 gun, and his evil ambitions grew.

The NYPD initially considered that the murder of Donna Lauria in July 1976 and the wounding of her friend, Jody Valenti, followed by non-fatal attacks on Carl Denaro and Rosemary Keenan and then Donna DeMasi and Joanne Lomino, were unrelated. While the victims in each case were all brunettes aged between 16 and 20, and the modus operandi of the shooter was similar – he had jumped out at the victims who were sitting in cars, shot at them, then run away – there was nothing else definitive to link the crimes.

But the attacks had still started a wave of panic – they were so random. Anyone might be next. Even New Yorkers, who were used to high crime rates, expected there to be some motivation for this sort of act. Terror swept the city. The *New York Post* ran a front-page headline declaring, "No One is Safe". Women started cutting their hair and wearing blonde wigs.

Then, in January 1977, another attack occurred and drew the focus of law enforcement. Christine Freund, 26, and her fiancé, John Diel, 30, were, like the other victims, sitting in their car. Freund, like all the other female victims, had dark hair. Again, the shooter came out of nowhere. Again, there was a survivor, Diel, who drove away. In all the cases .44 caliber bullets were used.

A month later another dark-haired woman, Virginia Voskerichian, 19, was walking home from Columbia University about a block from where Freund lived when a gunman approached and took aim. Voskerichian shielded herself with her textbooks, but the bullets went through them and killed her. The police reported that the bullets came from the same gun that had killed Lauria, the first victim.

A month later Alexander Esau, 20, a tow truck operator, and Valentina Suriani, 18, a Lehman College student and aspiring model, sat in their car a few blocks from the first shooting. A nearby resident heard four shots and called the police. The pair were found dead, each with two .44 caliber bullets in the head.

But this time there was a difference. The killer had left a note. It told police that the writer had an imaginary father, Sam, and when Sam got drunk, he got mean. He loved to drink blood. And he would say to his son, according to the letter, "GO OUT AND KILL." The killer thus acquired a name: the "Son of Sam".

Son of Sam wrote a letter to a *Daily News* journalist, Jimmy Breslin. The letter was a violent rant which told of future killings. Someone had written on the back of the envelope, "Blood and Family – Darkness and Death – Absolute Depravity – .44".

Then, on 26 June 1977, Salvatore Lupo, 20, and Judy Placido, 17, sat in Lupo's car at 3 a.m. after leaving a disco in Queens. Three gunshots smashed into their vehicle. Both survived. Lupo later told police they had been discussing the Son of Sam.

A year and two days after the first killing, the final attack took place. Two 20-year-olds, secretary Stacy Moskowitz and clothing salesman Robert Violante, were kissing in a car when four bullets were shot into them. Violante survived, Moskowitz died. She had become the first blonde victim of the Son of Sam.

But this time the Son of Sam had been seen – a Ford Galaxie spotted near the final killing was traced and was found to have a series of strange letters, maps of crime scenes and a .44 calibre Bulldog pistol inside it. The car was owned by David Berkowitz. Police waited for him to go to his vehicle and pounced. Smiling, Berkowitz asked the police what had taken them so long. His apartment was full of Satanic symbols, and there was a diary that listed all his crimes, including, to the astonishment of law enforcement, a series of arsons.

And who was Sam? It turned out he was a former neighbour whose dog, Harvey, had become possessed by a demonic spirit. Berkowitz attempted to kill the dog, but supernatural influences prevented him. According to Berkowitz, it was Harvey who ordered Berkowitz to kill and who had made him the Son of Sam.

Berkowitz received six life sentences, or 365 years behind bars. During his sentencing, he chanted that Stacy was a whore, in reference to the last of his killings, and confessed to a number of other murders. His growing celebrity – and potential book deals – led to New York passing what is known as the Son of Sam Law, which stops criminals from profiting financially from their crimes.

He remains in prison and is now an Evangelical Christian who calls himself the Son of Hope. His remorse seems a little too late.

ADOLF EICHMANN

"The banality of evil." Written by the German philosopher Hannah Arendt, this is one of the great quotes of the twentieth century. As we have seen, many acts of evil have been far from banal, and yet, as in the case of the man Arendt was talking about, Adolf Eichmann, evil can be done simply by wielding a pen and obeying authority. As banal as that.

Adolf Eichmann was what we might now call a "middle manager," albeit one reasonably high up in the organization – and this organization was the Nazi Party. Essentially Eichmann was in charge of logistics, tasked with organizing the movement of goods from and to their final destination. But these goods were Jews, and the final destination – part of the Final Solution – was the gas chambers. It was a job he did as efficiently as possible, taking real pride in his work.

Born in Germany in 1906 to a middle-class family, Eichmann was a poor student – he attended the same school Adolf Hitler had 17 years earlier – and so was sent by his father to vocational college. He worked at his father's mining company, then as a sales clerk and finally for an oil company in Austria. He excelled in none.

Meanwhile, in 1932, he had joined the Nazi Party. When the oil company fired him, he moved back to Germany, devoted himself to Hitler's party and gradually rose through the ranks. In 1934, he joined a group reporting on Jewish organizations, and by 1938, he was working on ways to force all Jews to voluntarily emigrate from Germany.

Soon after, with the start of the Second World War, this became forced emigration. Eichmann found himself in charge of organizing these deportations – in the first year some 63,000 Jews were packed on trains to be taken away to concentration camps, with a third of them dying in transit.

Then, in January 1942, the leaders of the Nazi Party gathered in the Wannsee district of Berlin. The Wannsee Conference was to be one of the most chilling gatherings in history. Here the Nazi leaders discussed the logistics of completely eliminating Jews from the face of the Earth – what they called "The Final Solution". This task was given to Eichmann – he would organize the identification, assembly and transportation of Jews from everywhere in Europe to their final destinations at Auschwitz and other extermination camps.

Here Eichmann found his "calling". He did not make policy, but he made sure the policies given to him were carried out with ruthless efficiency and that no mercy was shown to the victims.

Eichmann and his underlings arranged the deportation of Jews from Slovakia, the Netherlands, France and Belgium, then Greece, Italy and Hungary. Men, women and children were packed into trains and delivered for execution – no one branded as Jewish by the Nazis would be allowed to survive. Eichmann's record-keeping was immaculate, and he stayed ahead of all quotas. Six million Jews died in the Holocaust – Eichmann was responsible for a huge quantity of them going to their deaths.

In 1944, with the war almost lost, he fled but was captured by US forces in 1945. He managed to escape and changed his identity, hiding in rural Germany even as his name often came up during the Nuremberg trials of Nazi war criminals, which took place from 20 November 1945 to 1 October 1946.

In 1950, he fled to Argentina, getting a job at Mercedes Benz, where he rose to be a department head. But Jewish Nazi hunters were on his trail, and on 11 May 1960, three Israeli Mossad agents captured him. He was taken to Jerusalem, and his trial, attended by Hannah Arendt, would be a sensation.

The prosecution case was presented over the course of 56 days, involving hundreds of documents and 112 witnesses (many of them Holocaust survivors). Arendt, among others, noted Eichmann's dry – boring, even – style of responding to questions. This was evil at its most banal, a series of evasions and statistics. He was a small, unimpressive man, carrying out great evil to terrible effect.

Eichmann claimed to have known little about what was going on – his constant response of "I was just following orders" has passed into the language as a phrase denoting someone evading responsibility. Previous interviews revealed he had indeed known everything that was happening and welcomed the eradication of the Jews.

The jury found him guilty and a true perpetrator of the genocide of the Jews, not merely as some functionary. On 15 December 1961, Eichmann was sentenced to death by hanging. Eichmann appealed, and there were further hearings during the first half of 1962. It was noted that fair trials were not something any of his victims received.

At 8 p.m. on 31 May 1962, his final appeal was rejected. Just after midnight the same day, he was taken to the gallows. He was, the executioner later noted, wearing chequered slippers as though he was just padding about his house, a final banal detail.

Although he didn't make the rules, Eichmann made sure they were carried out. His failure to resist is a lesson for us all. As Arendt put it, "The sad truth is that most evil is done by people who never make up their minds to be good or evil."

JOHN WAYNE GACY

He was born in Illinois in 1942 to an alcoholic father who physically abused both him and his sister, often beating the young boy and telling him he was dumb. Frequently hospitalized – he was both overweight and sickly – he missed a lot of schooling. According to him, as a young boy, a family friend would take him to his truck and force him to engage in sex acts. If we can locate the birth of evil in a man in his childhood, John Wayne Gacy could not have been better primed. He would become one of the most feared serial killers in history.

What set Gacy apart from other killers, and what made him a figure of terror among the general population of the time – and since – was that he carried out many of his crimes dressed as that creepiest of things.

A clown.

Coulrophobia – the fear of clowns – is said to affect 1 in 100 children. But it also affects one in ten adults. Why this is so remains a mystery, but the activities of Gacy during the 1970s may well be a contributing factor.

Escaping from his family at the age of 20 and moving to Las Vegas, Gacy briefly worked as an ambulance driver. But then he found a job that suited his interests better. He started working at a mortuary. For three months he was an attendant in the embalming room, watching corpses be prepared for burial. One night, he later told police, he climbed into one of the coffins and cuddled up to a dead male teenager. Shocked at himself, he fled and quit the job soon after, returning to Illinois. This was, he later said, the happiest time in his life. He married, became a respected member of a number of community groups and rose to a management position at KFC. He had two children. But beneath this rosy surface, frustration and anger were brewing and would soon land him in trouble.

Gacy was a closeted gay person at a time when gay acts were illegal, and in 1968, he was charged with sodomy, receiving his first jail sentence. He lost his job, and his wife left him, taking the children. And he was forced to undergo psychological testing – same-gender sexual orientation was not only regarded as a sin but as a mental illness. The test diagnosed him as having psychopathic traits.

On release he got a job in construction. But as he later acknowledged, his sexual desires had become more urgent, and he engaged in a series of sexual assaults. He also began a second line of work – he performed as a clown at children's parties. Gacy had two characters he dressed as – Pogo and Patches. Pogo was, Gacy would later say, the "happy clown". Patches was "more serious".

In 1971, he married again, and after a short while, he told his wife he was bisexual. He started staying out late in the evening, and she saw him go into the garage with teenage boys. She later found gay porn and a number of wallets. She never saw the boys leave and assumed they did after she was asleep. In 1976, she was granted a divorce on grounds of infidelity.

It was in 1978 that 15-year-old Robert Piest went missing. Police were informed that the teenager had gone to see Gacy about a job, and they grew suspicious. Gacy's house was searched, but astonishingly nothing was found. Still, they took Gacy in for questioning. He told them he had never met Piest. Knowing this was a lie, they decided to search the house more thoroughly, this time tearing into the walls.

What the police found would shock the world. In the crawl space of Gacy's house were the remains of what turned out to be at least 29 victims, all of them young men, in various states of decomposition. The teenagers he lured into his garage had not, in fact, left. They had been sexually assaulted, tortured and then killed. So badly were they decomposed that police took months to identify how many of them there were, let alone who they were. He had also used quicklime to dissolve a number of bodies.

Gacy admitted to 30 murders, but he couldn't remember all the names, so there may have been more. He didn't kill them, he said, until they begged him to do so to stop the suffering. Then he would put a wire around their necks with a hammer through it, which he would turn until the wire tightened and they died. Later, he started killing them by shoving paper or plastic down their throats.

His usual method was to lure the teenagers back to his garage with promises of drugs and alcohol. He would then handcuff them, pretending it was part of a magic trick he did when clowning. He then proceeded to rape and torture them, including pressing foreign objects into them, all while taunting them. Some he held under water in his bath, pulling them out again and again before they drowned, before finally finishing them off.

By the time of his trial, 33 victims had been identified. At the trial he claimed to have a number of personalities, not only the two clowns but also a police officer called Jack Hanley, whom he referred to as "Bad Jack", who Gacy said detested gay people. The defence tried an insanity plea, but this was rejected on the grounds that the killings had been meticulously planned, and he had covered them up just as meticulously.

The jury found him guilty of all 33 murders, the most in US history to that date, and he received 33 death sentences. His execution was set for late 1980, but various appeals and delays meant that it was not until 9 May 1994 that he was given a fatal injection. Outside the prison a crowd of over 1,000 people gathered to cheer on the killing. Many of them wore T-shirts that read "No Tears for the Clown". None were shed.

DENNIS NILSEN

He himself complained about the blocked drains.

When the residents of the Cranley Gardens apartments in Muswell Hill, London, complained about the plumbing, it was Dennis Nilsen who wrote the letter to the estate agents. He was there when plumber Michael Cattran opened the drain cover and saw, to his revulsion, what seemed to be flesh. Nilsen said he thought maybe someone had been flushing fried chicken through the drains.

They hadn't. These were, in fact, the human remains Nilsen himself had been flushing down the toilet. If he failed to make the connection, it may be because the flesh he was disposing of was only a minor part of the horrific crimes he was committing in his apartment. Most of the remains of his victims he kept. Initially he placed them under the floorboards; he would later dissect them, put them in plastic bags and store them about the apartment. Heads, hands and feet he boiled to remove the flesh. It was this flesh he poured down the toilet.

Born in 1945 in Scotland to a Norwegian soldier and a woman from Aberdeenshire, Dennis Nilsen served in the army between 1961 and 1972. Discharged, he joined the police force but resigned a year later, believing his lifestyle in the London gay scene and his job were incompatible. He then worked for an employment agency, where he was a conscientious employee, rising through the ranks until his arrest.

It was on 30 December 1978, while living in Cricklewood, that he first killed. He had met 14-year-old Stephen Holmes at a pub, trying to buy alcohol. He invited Holmes home, thinking he was 17. The pair spent the night drinking. In the morning when he woke, Nilsen found the boy asleep beside him. Nilsen stated he was afraid to wake him in case he left. He wanted to keep him. So he strangled him with his necktie, then drowned him in a bucket of water. He then took the body to bed and masturbated on it. When rigor mortis set in, he placed the body under the floorboards, burning it on a bonfire eight months later.

It was a year before he killed again, a 23-year-old Canadian student named Kenneth Ockenden. The pattern was similar: this time Nilsen used a headphone cord to strangle his victim, took Polaroids of the body in sexual positions and, after placing him beneath the floorboards, took him out again four times to keep him company. It was the same with his next victim, 16-year-old Martyn Duffey, on 17 May 1980, who he stored in the cupboard. When the body started to bloat, he put it beneath the floorboards too.

After Duffey's death the frequency of Nilsen's murders increased: he committed another five before the end of 1980. By now the smell from under the floorboards was becoming impossible to live with. Nilsen dissected the maggot-ridden bodies, built a fire in his yard and burned them, throwing on a tyre to disguise the smell. He remembered local children coming to watch the fire and wished they would dance around the mass funeral pyre.

Soon after, he moved to 23D Cranley Gardens, an attic flat – there were no floorboards for storing bodies. It was not until March 1982 that he killed again, this time 23-year-old John Howlett, who he strangled and drowned in a bathtub. Three months later he killed 27-year-old Graham Allen. As with Howlett, Nilsen then dissected him on the kitchen floor and stored his remains about the apartment. And flushed some flesh down the toilet.

It was 26 January 1983, a week before he wrote to the estate agent, that Nilsen killed his final victim, 20-year-old Stephen Sinclair. The pair consumed lots of drugs and alcohol. Nilsen knelt before Sinclair and said he was sorry, but he couldn't help himself. The day after the letter to the estate agent, Nilsen denied a friend access to the apartment. The body was still on the kitchen floor, being dismembered.

When the plumber returned the day after his initial visit, the drain had been cleared, but he did find four bones which were obviously human. The drain was directly from Nilsen's apartment. That evening when Nilsen returned from work, the police were waiting. They informed him they were there about the drains, and he asked why the police would be interested. On being informed about the human remains, Nilsen pretended to be surprised.

But when the police entered his apartment, the odour of death was overwhelming. Asked where the other remains were, he directed them to the kitchen cupboards. He was asked if they were the remains of one person or two. Nilsen replied that there were 15 or 16 since 1978.

In 1983, Nilsen was sentenced to life imprisonment with a recommendation that he serve a minimum of 25 years. In 1994, this was extended to a whole-life tariff, ensuring he would never be released.

The apartment at 23D Cranley Gardens was bought by a property developer, who refurbished it completely but was unable to sell it for many years, perhaps due to the property listing: "Buyers are kindly asked to research the history of this property or enquire with the marketing agent prior to viewings."

GARY RIDGWAY

Gary Ridgway began killing women in 1982, and he was one of the most prolific serial killers in history. In all, he was charged with 49 murders, and it is believed that 43 of them happened in the two years after his first. All of the women had been raped. His wives later told police that his sexual appetites were unquenchable, and he often required sex several times a day from them. He would then still go out and look for more, frequently visiting prostitutes, who he resented for taking his money.

His method was almost always the same – he would pick the victims up on a small stretch of the Pacific Highway South, sometimes showing them a picture of his young son Matthew to win their trust. Once he had them alone, he would engage in sexual intercourse from the rear, strangling them as he did.

In the beginning he dumped their bodies in the Green River in Washington, earning the nickname the Green River Killer. But disposing of the bodies meant they could not be used again, so soon after he changed tactics, keeping the bodies and engaging in necrophilia. He did this, he told police, not because he enjoyed having sex with corpses – in fact, it disgusted him – but in order to stop himself from having to kill again. Later he started burying bodies – this time to stop himself having sex with them.

Born in 1949, Ridgway had been a troubled child with an IQ of only 82, who delighted in shooting birds – cruelty to animals is common in those who later graduate to cruelty to humans. In 1963, at the age of 14, he attempted to kill a six-year-old boy, taking him into the woods and stabbing him a number of times, both through the ribs and into the liver. The boy survived somehow, and Ridgway was never charged. He would later claim he had killed a boy as a teenager by holding him under water, although no proof was ever found.

He was married twice, and both wives left him because of his extramarital affairs. During his second marriage he became very religious, reading aloud from the Bible at work and home and going from door-to-door preaching.

By 1982, twice divorced, he was working in a factory spray-painting trucks. He was seen as a loner, and his workmates started jokingly calling him Green River Gary when the first five dead bodies were found. Arrested for visiting prostitutes and causing them bodily harm, he was actually questioned about the murders, but no link could be found. The killings continued, and the community in the area was traumatized as so many women went missing.

Then, in 1985, the killing suddenly stopped. The police were baffled. Had the killer just moved on? Been caught for another crime? Died? There were no clues.

In fact, what had happened was that Ridgway had met a woman and fallen in love. Judith Mawson became his third wife and was able to satisfy his urges. In fact, according to Ridgway, he killed only three of his victims after they married – one in each of 1987, 1990 and 1998.

Mawson later said that the two were compatible physically, intellectually, financially and socially, and they shared cute rituals and hobbies. She also said that she had never heard of the Green River Killer when she met Ridgway, saying, "I feel I have saved lives... by being his wife and making him happy."

Meanwhile, the police investigation progressed. First, the police received a letter offering to help solve the crime – from Ted Bundy, then six years into his own sentence for serial killing. Bundy had figured out that the Green River Killer was going back to have intercourse with the corpses and suggested staking out the next one they found rather than retrieving it. The chief inspector on the case had no doubt about Bundy's true motive – "It was as if Mr Bundy was jealous of the attention the Green River Killer was getting," he said.

Executed in 1989, Bundy would not live to see Ridgway arrested, but his assistance was vital in coming up with a profile of the killer – getting inside his mind. However, it was a different development that would finally lead to the police catching up with the Green River Killer – a new form of testing crime scenes and victims. DNA.

Back in 1987, police got a lead that every time a woman disappeared, Gary Ridgway had been absent from work. They searched his house and took samples of his hair and saliva. But the evidence of his absences was circumstantial, and no technology existed to match him to the murders. When the killings seemed to stop, the case was declared cold.

But a new test in 2001 revealed that the DNA of semen taken from a dead woman matched with that of Ridgway's saliva. Four other women were tested, with the same result. Ridgway was immediately arrested and charged with five murders. Under questioning he confessed to another and another – 48 in total.

Tried in 2003, he was spared the death penalty as part of a plea bargain – he would show the police where all the missing bodies were in exchange for his life. He received 48 life sentences, with another one added in 2011 when another victim was found – he apologized for losing count. He later claimed that there were, in fact, 65 victims, and then 71. Then over 80. We may never know the true figure, but we do know that when asked why he did it, Ridgway said it was simple – killing was his career.

SHIRŌ ISHII

It was called Unit 731 and was a part of the Imperial Japanese Army, in commission from 1936 to 1945. But behind the mundane name was one of the most horrifying creations in human history. Unit 731 was the home of the Japanese Army's biological warfare experiments. Both the US and Great Britain tested biological weapons during the Second World War, but their tests were on animal subjects, not humans. Unit 731, under its director Shirō Ishii, had no such ethical scruples. He was developing poisons to kill humans – so he would test them on humans.

Estimates vary on how many humans suffered at the hands of Ishii and his team of 3,000, but we do know it was over 14,000 – mostly civilians and Chinese or Allied prisoners of war. They were forced to ingest, or have injected into them, some of the deadliest pathogens known to humanity – pathogens which caused such diseases as anthrax, gangrene, smallpox, botulism, tuberculosis, tetanus, cholera, encephalitis, salmonella and dysentery. Others were forced to give each other syphilis by being made to engage in sexual contact.

In most cases, the victims did not die of the disease – they were murdered first so that an autopsy could be carried out to check the progress of the pathogen or the illness through the body. Some, however, were "taken to term" – after a long, horrible death they were also tested. Ishii also carried out a huge number of vivisections on living victims – without anaesthetic. He filmed much of his work for reference.

He was in no doubt about what he was doing. If the aim of medicine were to prevent and cure disease, his work, he said openly, was the complete opposite of these principles. In the lab he was slovenly dressed, with his lab coat often covered in bloodstains and cigarette ash. He was known as a heavy drinker, someone who regularly embezzled money and a womanizer. These sins were forgiven due to the brilliance of his scientific mind.

He had been born in 1892, the fourth son of Katsuya Ishii, a wealthy landowner and sake maker. He was blessed with a photographic memory and was a brilliant student, which instilled in him an arrogance his former classmates would always remember.

He became a medical scientist and then, in 1921, a military surgeon. By 1928, he had risen through the ranks, and he became an advocate of starting a biological weapons programme, having toured the West and seen the advances being made. A fervent nationalist, he was able to convince people at a prominent level in the government to support him and give him money. By 1935, he was the army's chief surgeon, and by 1936, he had been given formal control over Unit 731 and its research facilities.

Euphemistically called the "Anti-Epidemic Water Supply and Purification Bureau", Unit 731 gave Ishii complete power over

Japan's biochemical research, and he used that power fully. He recruited the brightest medical students, scientists, researchers and staff that Imperial Japan had to offer, who helped him carry out his experiments in what was a true chamber of horrors.

But Ishii's immorality was not just confined to the lab. He masterminded two bubonic plague attacks on the Chinese cities of Changde and Ningbo, dropping 700 aerial bombs containing 70 kilograms of Salmonella typhi, 50 kilograms of Vibrio cholerae and 5 kilograms of plague fleas. Several thousand people died, and the cities ended up being walled off and burned to the ground to prevent the spread of the diseases.

He also planned an attack on the US, specifically the heavily populated cities of San Diego, Los Angeles and San Francisco. The attack was codenamed Operation Cherry Blossoms at Night. Planes would spread bubonic plague, cholera, typhus, dengue fever and other pathogens, while submarine crews would infect themselves and go ashore. The plan was shelved as the war drew to its end.

After the US victory, and knowing his activities constituted a war crime, Ishii faked his own death to avoid being executed. He need not have worried. When the US worked out he was still alive, they captured him, and he was interred at Fort Detrick in Maryland. Aware that the Soviets were making advances in chemical weapons, Ishii offered to turn over all of his data and knowledge to the Allies in return for immunity from prosecution. This deal was accepted – a "relatively cheap" price to pay for such "invaluable information", as army microbiologist Lieutenant Colonel Murray Sanders put it.

Ishii returned to Japan a free man and opened a clinic, performing examinations and treatments for free. He also attended a number of reunion parties for the staff at Unit 731. He was never cited for war crimes.

According to his daughter, just before he died in 1959, he converted to Roman Catholicism. It is not known whether he attended confession regularly.

DAVID PARKER RAY

In the end, he was never charged with murder. He was convicted for the kidnapping and torture of just three women, Cynthia Vigil, Angelica Montano and Kelli Garrett, receiving a sentence of 224 years. He died of a heart attack after only one year in prison, leaving 223 years unserved. David Parker Ray does not make any list of murderers, let alone serial killers. And yet no one is in any doubt that he was one. And that the number of victims was at least 60, possibly over 100.

He was known as the Toy Box killer, but there was nothing cute about the toy box – it was his nickname for his utility trailer, parked in his yard in Elephant Butte, New Mexico, which he had soundproofed and kitted out with items for sexual torture, including surgical instruments, chains, pulleys, straps, clamps, spreader bars, syringes, electroshock devices and diagrams of the human body, as well as a gynaecological table onto which he could strap his victim. There was also a mirror mounted on the ceiling so that the victims could see everything being done to them.

His method was usually the same. He would kidnap a woman and keep her prisoner either for a few days or, in some cases, for two to three months. A number of accomplices would join in, including his partner and one of his daughters. Their dog was also used. Then he would either kill his victim or drug them with barbiturates in an attempt to erase their memories of what had happened before abandoning them by the side of the road.

He also videotaped what he did. This would be crucial in his capture.

Ray was born in 1939 in New Mexico. His father was an alcoholic, and Ray and his sister were brought up by his mother's parents. His father would visit sometimes, sharing sadomasochistic pornography with him. By the age of 14, Ray was drawing his own sadomasochistic images, and in a 1993 recording, he said he first committed rape even earlier. He also told his first wife that his first murder had happened in 1957 when he was 18.

On the same tape he claimed that he had already had 37 victims, although without specifying if he had killed them. A mechanic, he had already made his torture chamber and adapted many tools to use in his assaults. By then his partner, Cindy Hendy, was involved – victims would also be forced to serve her, as well as his daughter Jesse, who would help lure victims back to her father.

It was on 22 March 1999 that a woman, Cynthia Vigil, was found running down a road in Elephant Butte wearing only a slave collar and chains. She was taken to the police, and she told them how she had escaped from David Parker Ray. A search of his house revealed a number of torture devices. And then they found the trailer. There was no doubt that Vigil was telling the truth and that the truth was more terrible than the police had dared to imagine.

The problem was that Vigil was a prostitute and drug addict and therefore unlikely to be believed in court. But there was a tape which showed a woman being used. She had a tattoo, and police were able to make a public plea for information. The tattoo belonged to Kelli Garrett, a friend of Ray's daughter. He had abused Garrett for three days, memories she had repressed until she saw the tattoo. She agreed to give evidence.

Based on statements in the videotapes, the police had little doubt Ray was a killer – women linked to him had gone missing. But Ray lived near both a national park and a lake – easy places to hide bodies. Every piece of evidence led to a dead end. Even when one accomplice, his so-called "playmate" Dennis Yancy, was found guilty of one murder, which he said Ray had ordered, and sentenced to 20 years in prison, there was still nothing that firmly implicated Ray. Only the word of a murderer.

The police decided to try him for kidnapping and rape only, beginning with that of Kelli Garrett. The first trial ended as a mistrial – two of the jurors did not believe that the sex was non-consensual. But a retrial saw him convicted. He then entered a plea during the case of Cynthia Vigil to make sure his daughter was not jailed. He was sentenced to 224 years in prison. Cindy Hendy received 36 years.

No victims were ever found. They remain missing persons.

CHRISTMAN GENIPPERTEINGA

Did he exist? There are those who say not, that he is a figment of a German imagination that likes its folktales and stories of the macabre. Certainly, he shares some characteristics of other ancient German villains, robbers and cannibals, and the sources available are scant and dubious. But then so is so much from the sixteenth century. Perhaps the best we can say is that if Christman Genipperteinga didn't exist, someone would have had to invent him, and perhaps that is bad enough.

He was, according to contemporary reports, born in Kerpen, a small town near Cologne in Germany, at an unknown date. Of his childhood and early adulthood, we know very little, but we do know that by 1569, he was living in a cave a mile from the town of Bergkessel. He began as a highway robber, preying on any travellers who happened to pass the cave. But he soon graduated to much greater evil.

He is said to have kidnapped a woman named Dorothea from nearby Boppard, keeping her as a sex slave and fathering six children with her – all of which he killed. Legend had it he ate their hearts, hanged the corpses on a tree outside and when the wind made their corpses move, he would cry out that they were dancing.

The killing of his children gave him a taste for murder and, if the records are to be believed, for eating human flesh. With Dorothea chained in his cave, he would bring back more and more victims – Dorothea would tell the authorities he was killing daily at the height of his madness.

In May 1581, Dorthea pleaded with Genipperteinga to be allowed to travel to see her relatives in Trier. He agreed if she swore an oath not to betray him – to break an oath at that time was to condemn the oath breaker to hell. Dorothea agreed and went, holding her peace for as long as she could.

But when she saw all the children of Trier, she could not help but remember her own dead sons and daughters. Visibly upset, she collapsed in the street. She would tell no one what was wrong, until a priest promised her that she would not go to hell if she told him. She did.

The authorities let her return alone so as not to alert Genipperteinga. Then, on 27 May, they descended. There they found Genipperteinga unconscious – Dorothea had used a drug on him supplied to her by the authorities. They also found an immense amount of loot in the form of wine, salted meat, suits of armour, weaponry, coins and other valuables.

Genipperteinga immediately confessed – including his own children, he had killed 964 men, women and children, making him one of history's greatest serial killers. He had kept a diary describing each death. His only regret, he said, was that he had not reached his goal of 1,000 murders.

On 17 June 1581, he was found guilty and sentenced to be tortured to death. He lasted nine days before perishing by being broken on a wheel – a large, spoked wheel was moved over his body again and again, breaking all his bones and tearing off his flesh.

Of the diary, no trace was ever found – some say it was burned by the authorities, worried that the crimes of Genipperteinga would inspire what we would nowadays call copycats. Others say that there was no diary, it was just an invention of those who wished to terrify others. But a final theory says it is out there somewhere, a collection of depravities to match those of the Marquis de Sade's novels. Except, of course, the Marquis de Sade only imagined his crimes – they weren't real…

MARTIN BRYANT

It would be wrong to say that the photograph was the most shocking thing about it – after all, he had killed 35 people in cold blood and injured another 23 in the sort of rampage unheard of in Australia, let alone Tasmania, generally regarded as one of the friendliest, most laid-back places in the country. It was assumed that the killer would resemble some sort of commando – be dressed in battle fatigues, look strong, perhaps with a shaved head and tattoos.

Instead, when the first pictures of Martin Bryant were released, what people saw was an angelic-looking young man with curly blonde locks, slim and obviously shy. When it emerged that he had also inherited a large fortune, the sense of bewilderment only increased.

Later, the facts of Bryant's life would reveal that the man who carried out the mass shooting was not all he seemed from those first pictures. Martin Bryant was a very disturbed individual, and the murders were a culmination of a lifetime of angry and aggressive acts.

Born on 7 May 1967, he soon grew into a difficult and "annoying" child, according to his mother. At school he appeared distant and unemotional, and he was bullied by other children. He would sometimes act violently, torturing animals and, on one occasion, trying to drown a fellow student by pulling his snorkel away while diving. At 16, a psychiatric assessment showed that Bryant was disturbed and possibly schizophrenic. It also noted he had an IQ of 66, the equivalent of an 11-year-old.

In 1987, aged 19, he had met 54-year-old Helen Harvey, heiress to a share in the Tattersall's lottery fortune, who was then living in squalor with 14 dogs and 40 cats, and a sister who died soon after they met. In 1991, they moved in together, and Bryant was known to prowl their property, firing an airgun at dogs and sometimes at passing humans.

On 20 October 1992, Helen Harvey died in a car accident. Bryant was in the car and had a history of grabbing the wheel. Nothing could be proved, and he inherited over half a million dollars that she had left him in her will. The property also went to him, but his parents were given guardianship of the money due to his mental health, and his father moved in. A year later his father was also dead – his body was discovered in a dam close to the property, weighted down with a diving weight belt around the neck. It was ruled a suicide, and Martin Bryant inherited another $250,000.

All alone in the world, he started drinking heavily – and started to plan an act that would relieve him of all the anger building inside.

Port Arthur has long been a popular holiday destination in Tasmania, albeit with a somewhat shady past. From 1833, it had been a penal colony for British prisoners shipped to Australia, and it was a notorious convict settlement for the most hardened criminals, some of whom had been moved there from other prisons that were unable to cope. For this reason, it was also one of the strictest of the prisons, and despite having a large population of child convicts, all were expected to do hard labour under threat of severe punishment.

But after the prison was shut down, Port Arthur gradually evolved, eventually becoming a tourist destination. By 1979, it had been turned into one of the most popular destinations in Australia, with picnic areas, woodland walks, and cafés and shops.

It was approximately 1.10 p.m. on 28 April 1996, a beautiful spring day, when Bryant pulled his yellow Volvo into the parking lot of Port Arthur. He had, it would later be revealed, already killed two people that morning – David and Noelene Martin, who had bought a house Bryant's father had also bid on before he died. Bryant shot them dead in their home and drove on to Port Arthur.

There he paid the entrance fee and went to the café, which was full of people. Bryant was carrying what the café owner called a "sports-type bag". He appeared nervous and made attempts at small talk with the people around him.

Then he drew an AR-15 rifle from the bag and shot the two people at the table next to his. The Port Arthur Massacre had begun.

In the next 15 seconds, Bryant fired 17 times, killing 12 people and wounding ten more. He had placed himself by the exit so no one had been able to escape. He then left the café and walked toward the nearby gift shop. He also changed guns, now using an L1A1 SLR, a hugely powerful weapon usually used in combat. Entering the gift shop he continued firing. No one stood a chance. He fired 29 times, killing 20 people and wounding another 12.

By now people were fleeing the scene. Bryant paused in the gift shop to reload, then went out into the carpark, still firing, still killing. He walked to his car, shooting anyone who moved as he went. Getting in his Volvo, he saw Nanette Mikac and her children, Madeline, 3, and Alannah, 6, running from the site. He drove up to them and opened the door of the car. Mikac moved toward the car, thinking he might be trying to help her get away. Bryant leaped out, made her kneel, and then shot her. Then he shot the two little girls.

He killed the owners of a BMW, which he stole. Leaving the site, he drove to a petrol station nearby. There he stopped a white Toyota driven by Glenn Pears with Zoe Hall as his passenger. He dragged Pears from the car and forced him to get in the boot of the BMW. He shot Hall three times and drove the BMW back to the house where he had killed the Martins, firing at other cars as he did so. Parking up, he dragged Pears into the house and set light to the BMW.

Police swooped on the property, and a stand-off ensued, with Bryant using Pears as a hostage. Bryant's only demand was to be transported in an army helicopter to an airport – this was refused. The stand-off continued into the next day, during which time Bryant killed Pears. He then set light to the house and attempted to escape. He didn't succeed, and he received severe burns to his back and buttocks. He kept asking the police how many people had died.

He was charged with 35 counts of murder and found guilty of all of them, receiving 35 life sentences plus 1,035 additional years for attempted murder and inflicting grievous physical harm on numerous people, without the possibility of parole. His large inheritance was surrendered to the state. For the first eight months of his sentence, he was kept in solitary confinement for his own safety as much as that of his fellow prisoners. Transferred to a secure mental health unit, he attempted suicide twice in May 2007, but unlike most of those he shot, he survived, and at the time of writing is still incarcerated.

JOSEPH EDWARD DUNCAN

"The sun is brighter today, and my soul is lighter... The world is a more beautiful place without the evil that is Joseph Duncan." So said Diana Martinez on 28 March 2021. Duncan had died that day of a brain tumour, and Martinez, the mother of ten-year-old Anthony who had been murdered by Duncan on 4 April 1997, was holding nothing back. "God chose to make his end a long suffering, and I believe that is fitting. The horror of his thoughts consumed him."

Those thoughts had been with Joseph Edward Duncan a long time – according to him, at the age of 15, he had raped a nine-year-old at gunpoint, and later he claimed that by the time he was 16, he had raped at least 13 younger boys. By the time he died, he was known to have killed at least five and possibly eight people, as well as committing numerous rapes, kidnappings and acts of molestation. It was a life that few were unhappy to see end.

Born in 1963 in North Carolina, he was the fourth of five children born to Edward and Lillian Mae Duncan. His father was in the army, so the family moved often. His parents split up in 1979 when Joseph was 16. By then he had already carried out his first sex crimes – whether the numbers he would later confess to are accurate cannot be known. But in 1980, at the age of 17, he stole a cache of guns from his neighbour and abducted a 14-year-old boy, raping him at gunpoint. He was sentenced to 20 years in prison and served 14 before being released on parole.

The 14 years in prison had done nothing to change him, and it was not long after his release that he committed another series of horrific crimes. The first occurred in 1996 – on 6 July, two sisters, Sammiejo White, 11, and Carmen Cubias, 9, left the Crest Motel on Aurora Avenue in Seattle shortly before 11 p.m. to buy their older brother cigarettes. They never came back.

In February 1998, their bodies were discovered not far from the hotel, and it is believed they were murdered soon after they had been abducted. Duncan later confessed that he had killed them with a crowbar as revenge against the world for having been sent to jail.

Soon after, he spent a month in jail for marijuana use, as this had violated the terms of his parole. Once free, he again decided to take revenge against society, this time with ten-year-old Anthony Martinez. In April 1997, Anthony and his six-year-old brother Mark were playing outside when their father heard Mark yell, "They've got Tony!" Running outside, he found Mark by himself, and Tony was gone.

Mark would testify that a man had told them his cat was missing and asked them to help search for it. When the cat could not be found, the man drew a knife and tried to grab the younger boy. Tony got between them, so Duncan grabbed him instead and dragged him into his car. It was the last time he was ever seen. Duncan would later write that on that day his pain was gone, and all that was left was fear, which he liked better.

But it was eight years later that he would carry out the crime that landed him in jail for a third time. On 16 May 2005, the bodies of Brenda Groene, 40, her boyfriend, Mark McKenzie, 37, and her son, Slade Groene, 13, were found in their Idaho home, bludgeoned to death. Brenda's two other children, nine-year-old Dylan and eight-year-old Shasta, were missing. Their pictures appeared across national newspapers. Two weeks later Shasta was recognized at a restaurant with an unknown man. Police blocked off the exits and arrested the man without a struggle. It was Joseph Duncan.

They continued to search for Dylan, but two days later his remains were found in Montana. He had been shot in the head.

Shasta told authorities that Duncan had broken into their house in the middle of the night and was carrying a gun. He tied up Brenda, Mark and Slade, then took the two younger children outside. They heard a series of loud noises. He then took the two children away, telling them he had killed the others with a hammer. For the next six weeks he tortured and raped the pair of them, recording much of it on video.

According to Shasta, Duncan had killed Dylan by accident, his gun going off and hitting the boy in the stomach. She saw Dylan writhing on the ground, and then Duncan put the gun to his head and fired. Duncan started crying and told Shasta he was putting Dylan out of his misery. He later placed a noose around Shasta's neck and pulled, but when she told him to stop, he did.

On 18 January 2007, after protracted legal wranglings, Duncan was charged with "kidnapping, kidnapping resulting in death, aggravated sexual abuse of a minor, and sexual exploitation of a child resulting in death." He pleaded guilty to all charges. He also confessed to the killings of Sammiejo White, Carmen Cubias and Anthony Martinez, and he was given a life sentence on top of the death penalty. Jurors who had had to watch the videos of his crimes were offered counselling after the case.

In October 2020, while on Death Row, Duncan was diagnosed with a brain tumour. He declined any treatment, and on 28 March 2021, he died. Shasta Groene said, "For so long I have been struggling with hate towards that man. Today, I woke up feeling like my soul was finally free…"

YANG XINHAI

He had, he said, no desire to be part of society – society was not his concern. What he wanted was simple: he wanted to kill people. He wanted to rape women. And he wanted to be left alone to do so.

In the case of some criminals, especially serial killers, it is possible to delve into their past, find the whys, the wheres and the whens. Profiles can be built up, lessons learned. But sometimes the killer is only known through their crimes. Such is the case of Yang Xinhai. There is no Yang outside of his murders. He committed them every time he could, and we know of at least 67 murders and 23 rapes within the span of four years between 1999 and 2003. His crimes were always as brutal as possible. In one, for instance, he killed a father and a six-year-old girl with a shovel, then raped the pregnant wife of the man he had killed. We only know this from her testimony after she survived. What else he did, we can never know.

We can only look at the evidence – he murdered, without any sort of plan, in the provinces of Anhui, Hebei, Henan and Shandong in China. Breaking and entering at night, he killed rural villagers using axes, hammers and shovels. If there was a single man in the house, the single man would die; if there was a single woman, then she would too, usually after sexual abuse. If he found a family home, he would kill the family.

Born in 1968, he was known to be intelligent, but he dropped out of school at 17 and became a labourer. He was certainly smart enough to wear different-sized shoes to commit his crimes, meaning that it would be difficult to connect the crimes via the muddy footprints. His spree was not carried out in an animal frenzy. There was planning, and there was forethought. But was there any feeling of guilt?

No, he said, there wasn't.

And was there a motive? If there was, it was never known. And it cannot bring the 67 back to life or spare them their terrible final moments. He himself claimed he had no motive, although he also told police that his anger at the world had started when a girlfriend had left him because she found out he had spent time in labour camps after being found guilty of theft and rape. China's most prolific serial killer was executed by firing squad on Valentine's Day, 2014, aged 46.

CHARLES WHITMAN

All mass killings are disturbing, but there is something about the way Charles Whitman carried out his crime that is particularly unnerving. At 11.48 a.m. on a bright, clear morning on 1 August 1966, a pregnant 18-year-old student, Claire Wilson, and her fiancé, Thomas Eckman, were walking in a courtyard in the University of Texas at Austin when a bullet ripped into her abdomen, killing the unborn child instantly. Seconds later her boyfriend was shot in the head.

There was a brief pause, and then a number of other students also fell. At first, bystanders thought it may have been some sort of protest against the Vietnam War, but it soon became evident that the students were bleeding.

But where were the shots coming from? Within seconds, witnesses realized they were coming from the 28-storey Main Building tower at the university, and from the tower's observation deck. Someone was up there shooting, not just at students on the campus, but at others on nearby Guadalupe Street. Bodies were falling left, right and centre, struck by bullets which seemed to come out of thin air. The reach of the gun was tremendous – a 29-year-old electrical repairman, Roy Dell Schmidt, was shot nearly half a kilometre from the tower.

It only took four minutes for the police to arrive, but they were in an impossible situation. They had no way of getting to the shooter, and those who had already been hit but not killed could not be recovered from the line of fire. Some covering fire was provided to attempt to distract the shooter and, if they got lucky, hit him, but it seemed of little use.

Police even chartered a two-seater light aircraft, from which a sharpshooter named Marion Lee attempted to obtain a clear shot of Whitman as the aircraft orbited close to the tower, but without luck. Someone was going to have to climb the tower and find the shooter. Who, as it would turn out, was a former marine.

Charles Whitman was born in 1941 and suffered physical abuse at the hands of his father, an authoritarian who regularly beat his family. He was a gun collector and taught his children to use them when they were young. Whitman was hugely intelligent, played the piano and was a crack shot by the time he was 12.

After an incident following his graduation from high school, where his father had beaten him for getting drunk, Whitman joined the US Marines. His father attempted to stop him without success. He served for 18 months, from 1959 to 1960. He then enrolled in mechanical engineering on an army scholarship – at the University of Texas at Austin. In 1962, he married, and his future seemed bright.

But by 1966, he was seeking psychiatric help. His parents divorced in March of that year, his mother finally having had enough of the domestic abuse. His father phoned him daily to try and make him persuade his mother to return. Whitman also told the psychiatrist that he had struck his own wife twice and felt self-loathing for doing so, terrified that he was turning into his father.

On 31 July, the day before the shootings, he had written two suicide notes, in which he also wrote that he intended to kill both his mother and his wife before he killed himself to spare them the humiliation of what he was going to do. Friends who saw him that evening said that he looked like a weight had lifted from him, "You know, as if he'd solved a problem."

Just after midnight he drove to his mother's house on Guadalupe Street and stabbed her to death before placing her body on her bed and covering her with sheets. He left one of the suicide notes beside her. At 3 a.m., he arrived home and stabbed his wife to death in their bed.

He spent the rest of the night filling his footlocker with guns, coffee, vitamins, binoculars, a machete, a radio, toilet paper, a razor and a bottle of deodorant. He then dressed as a janitor and headed into the university. He entered the tower at 11.30 a.m. – police believe he wanted to maximize the deaths by timing his shooting to coincide with the 11.45 a.m. student class changeover.

On the way up the tower, he encountered 51-year-old receptionist Edna Townsley – who was, it was later revealed, supposed to be having a day off but was covering for a friend. Whitman bludgeoned her to death with his rifle butt. He then proceeded to the 28th floor observation deck and set up his equipment. And at 11.48 a.m., he started shooting.

Three police officers, Day, Martinez and McCoy, and a civilian, former Air Force tail gunner Allen Crum, made it to the tower and began to ascend, seeing dead and injured people on their way up. The ascent was long and arduous, and it was not until 1.24 p.m., over an hour and a half after the shooting began, that they reached the observation deck. The foursome broke onto the observation deck from two directions, and it was McCoy who shot Whitman several times between the eyes. Martinez then fired a direct shotgun blast into Whitman's left arm at point-blank range. The police briefly continued to fire at the tower, almost hitting Martinez, until Crum waved a white handkerchief.

Whitman had killed 15 people from the observation deck, including his first victim, the unborn baby, and wounded another 31 others. It was the first time a killing had happened "in real time" in the US media, and interest throughout and after was intense. Friends, family and police were interviewed about what had happened. An autopsy of Whitman revealed a brain tumour, and some, including his wife's father, thought this was the cause of his rage.

But perhaps the most chilling testimony came from a friend who had been at university with Whitman. He remembered the fellow mechanical engineering student looking up at the tower and saying to him that "a person could stand off an army from atop of [the Main Building's tower] before they got him."

H. H. HOLMES

The life of any serial killer is, by definition, built on secrets and lies – it does not do to tell anyone what you are up to. Added to that, the fear they inspire in the world can lead to the stories we tell about them becoming ever more lurid and fantastic. Separating fact from fiction becomes difficult. And in the case of someone like H. H. Holmes, it becomes impossible.

What we do know is that he was a con artist, a forger, a bigamist and a horse thief. We also know that he was a murderer. But whether he killed one person (as he was charged with), nine (as he was suspected of), 27 (as he confessed to) or 200 (as the newspapers of the time speculated), we will never know. Holmes built his career on falsehoods and hyperbole, and his legend contains plenty of both.

He is most famous for what became known as the "Murder Castle" in Chicago, which he was said to have used as the name suggests. The three-storey building was equipped with trapdoors, soundproof rooms, secret passageways, gas jets to asphyxiate victims, doors that could be locked from the outside and a kiln to cremate bodies. Or was it? Again, this may all be an exaggeration, either by Holmes, the police, or that old friend, rumour.

He was born, we are pretty sure, Herman Webster Mudgett on 16 May 1861, descended from the first English settlers of New Hampshire. His father was a drunk and a bully, but Holmes – as he renamed himself as an adult – proved himself a highly intelligent boy, excelling at school. This led to further bullying, including an incident where classmates forced him to place a skeleton's hands on his face. Terrified at the time, Holmes would later claim that the experience had made him obsessed with death, and soon after, he began killing and dissecting animals.

He enrolled in medical college in New Hampshire, and on graduation in 1884, he started working in an anatomy lab under Professor William James Herdman. At the time, anatomists sometimes indulged in graverobbing in order to have bodies to study. It is believed that Herdman did such a thing, and that Holmes joined him in his graverobbing forays. But his penchant for fraud was already there – Holmes later confessed to swindling insurance companies by presenting dead bodies, although how he did it, he kept secret.

It was in 1886 that he moved to Chicago and took the name H. H. Holmes. He found a job as a pharmacist working for Dr Elizabeth Holton, eventually taking over the business (rumour had it that he killed Holton, but this is false – she lived a long and happy life). It was on an empty lot across the road from the pharmacy that he had his purpose-built house erected.

He had arrived in Chicago just before it was, for a time, the biggest tourist destination in the world. The 1893 World's Fair saw around 27 million visitors arrive in Chicago between May and October. It would appear slightly fewer than that number left, all due to H. H. Holmes.

It is said that he would lure tourists to his house and then kill them in order to sell their skeletons to a nearby medical research facility. According to his confession, his favoured method of murder was suffocation, although he was happy to use starvation or immolation if necessary. One had to be careful with the latter not to destroy every part of the victim, thus eliminating its on-sale potential.

While all of this was going on, Holmes was continuing to defraud organizations. In 1893, he was arrested for insurance fraud after a fire at his home, but he was soon released. He also kept getting married. Back in New Hampshire in 1878, he married Clara Lovering and had a son, then left without divorcing her. In 1886, he married Myrta Belknap and had a daughter, and then, in 1894, he married Georgiana Yoke in Colorado on a brief visit.

It was in mid-1894 that he came up with a scheme that would lead to his capture. He convinced an associate who had helped with other criminal schemes, Benjamin Freelon Pitezel, to fake his own death in a pretend lab explosion after taking out a $10,000 insurance policy, which Holmes would then collect.

Pitezel took out the policy, but then Holmes had a better, simpler idea – he killed Pitezel instead, knocking him unconscious and setting him alight, and then collected the policy. He convinced Pitezel's wife to give her children, 13-year-old Alice, nine-year-old Nellie and seven-year-old Howard, into his care to travel to Canada, claiming he would take them to meet up with Pitezel. On 25 October, he murdered Alice and Nellie by locking them in a trunk, drilling a hole in the lid and pumping gas in through a hose. He then buried them in his new house in Toronto.

By now the police were on his trail, and Frank Geyer of the Philadelphia Police Department identified the Toronto house. Entering when Holmes was out, he was instantly alerted by the smell and went down to the cellar and started digging. In Geyer's words, "The deeper we dug, the more horrible the odour became, and when we reached the depth of three feet, we discovered what appeared to be the bone of the forearm of a human being." Holmes was long gone.

But not for long. Holmes was traced to Boston, where he was arrested and held on a charge of horse theft, while other evidence was gathered. Holmes confessed to 27 murders in Chicago, Indianapolis and Toronto, and six attempted murders. Some of those he claimed to have killed were very much alive, adding another layer of mystery.

In the end, Holmes was put on trial for the murder of Benjamin Pitezel only. He was found guilty and sentenced to death. On 7 May 1896, he was led to the gallows. It is said he remained calm and talkative. The drop did not kill him – he twitched on the end of the rope for 15 minutes. At his request, the coffin was set in concrete before burial to stop other graverobbers. It was dug up once in 2017 when a rumour spread that he had escaped execution. His body was perfectly preserved, even his moustache.

The Murder Castle was burned down by vigilantes in 1895. On the site now is a post office, with no secret passages.

CULT
LEADERS AND
MANIPULATORS

From the outside, it can appear incomprehensible. Who are these men that they can command such loyalty, that they can make intelligent people sacrifice themselves to someone else – who, quite often, is as mundane as the next man?

People speak of charisma, and perhaps it is as simple as that. To be a cult leader, one must have an idea, a goal, a dream. In a world where such things can be in short supply, perhaps this is attraction enough. The desire for a life that is meaningful can take any of us on a path that, to others, seems absurd.

And for the leaders themselves, the adoration of a growing circle of devotees can take a mild case of narcissism and amplify it exponentially. Believing you are Jesus reincarnated is a difficult piece of mental acrobatics; believing it when others agree with you can only reinforce your idea.

The men in these pages took this relationship and perverted it for their own ends. Murderers, rapists, torturers – any relationship they had with the moral world was destroyed in their encounter with the devotion of believers, and the devotion of their own hearts. A Stalin or a Hitler lived in the hearts of many of these men. We can only think the world lucky that their number of followers was often small and the extent of their crimes kept in some sort of check.

But that will be of little consolation to their victims.

CHARLES MANSON

Ask anyone about cult leaders, and there is one name that will always come up. Has anyone ever fit the nightmarish definition of "cult leader" more than Charles Manson? His wild staring eyes, his unkempt hair and beard. And of course, that swastika tattooed into the middle of his forehead. Even 50 years after he was thrown in prison for life, and many years after his 2017 death, Charles Manson continues to live in our heads as a terrifying example of the depths of human depravity.

To write the story of Manson would take a whole book – in fact, many have been written, and many more will follow. This was a man who convinced his followers to murder seven people in cold blood and may have been responsible for up to 28 more deaths through persuasion. He wanted a race war, and some hold him responsible for bringing the Summer of Love to a violent end. Even his most ardent followers were subjected to physical and mental torture that would haunt them for the rest of their lives.

He was born in 1934, and by the time he started his cult, the Manson Family, he had already been in prison twice, the first time at 17 for raping a boy at knifepoint, among other charges, and the second for forging checks, pimping a 16-year-old girl and robbery. Released in 1967, aged 25, he headed to Los Angeles and then San Francisco, where the Summer of Love was in full swing. Immediately becoming engaged in the counterculture, he moved to the hippy Haight-Ashbury district and started taking LSD and engaging in free love.

He gradually started to gain followers attracted to his charisma and his strange philosophy, which combined Jesus, the Beatles, LSD and Dale Carnegie's book *How to Win Friends and Influence People*. As he later admitted, he was very good at preying on the emotionally vulnerable, especially women.

He kept his followers dosed up on large quantities of LSD and engaged in perverse sexual practices, forcing them to submit to his desires and his will. His parole officer helped him obtain drugs, and he grew his number of followers, encouraging them to commit robberies. He also acted as a pimp for a number of his female followers, who would have sex in order to fund the Family.

The Family moved to a ranch in California, with Manson making some of his followers have sex with the blind 80-year-old owner as payment. By now the Family was a doomsday cult, with Manson predicting a race war. He believed that the Beatles song "Helter Skelter", ostensibly about a child's slide, predicted this war. In early 1969, he told his followers that Helter Skelter would start that summer and they should be prepared for combat with "the Blacks".

It was in August of that year that the Manson Family committed the crime that would make headlines across the world. Manson ordered four of his followers, one man and three women, to break into 10050 Cielo Drive in Beverly Hills, where he knew that the actress Sharon Tate, wife of the director Roman Polanski, was staying with friends. There, he told them, they were to destroy everyone present and make it as gruesome as possible.

Tate was eight and a half months pregnant at the time. The followers brutally killed four others who were there, stabbing them between 26 and 51 times. Tate pleaded to be allowed to stay alive, offering herself as a hostage until her child was born. It was to no avail. They stabbed her 16 times and then hung her with a nylon rope. An autopsy showed she was still alive when she was hanged.

The next night the same four, plus Manson and another two followers, went to the home of 44-year-old supermarket executive Leno LaBianca and his 43-year-old wife, Rosemary LaBianca, co-owner of a dress shop, where Manson had attended a party a year earlier. Manson had not felt the previous night's murders had been violent enough and supplied the killers with more powerful weapons, including a bayonet. He left them to their "work", killing the LaBiancas in a brutal attack. "Helter Skelter" was written on the refrigerator in their blood.

Two weeks later, on 26 August 1969, the Manson Family also killed Hollywood stuntman Donald Shea, who they believed had tipped police off about their involvement in the Tate murders. He was stabbed and brutally tortured to death.

By now the police had connected the Tate murders with the LaBianca ones, and over the course of the next three months, Manson and the followers involved were arrested. They were originally charged with seven counts of murder and one of conspiracy. Manson chose to act as his own attorney, constantly disrupting the proceedings.

In his defence, Manson said he was not to blame, as he didn't write the music which had predicted the slayings – he was just a conduit. Manson and his followers were sentenced to death, later commuted to life imprisonment when the death penalty was abolished. In prison, he was convicted of two more murders, including that of Donald Shea.

The Manson Family had not finished wreaking havoc – on 5 September 1975, another follower, Lynette "Squeaky" Fromme, attempted to assassinate US president Gerald Ford to show her devotion to Manson. The gun failed to go off. Fromme was incarcerated and swore her allegiance to Manson, insisting she was in love with him.

In prison, Manson continued to cause trouble, racking up 108 code violations. He gave television interviews in which he expressed no remorse and continued to insist on his mission. He lived until 19 November 2017, when he died from colon cancer. He remains an inspiration for neo-Nazi groups in the US, who are waiting for the race war he prophesized.

JIM JONES

"Drinking the Kool-Aid" – the phrase has passed into popular culture to mean someone who has fallen for a foolish or deranged concept or ideology, usually some sort of conspiracy theory, political belief or religious faith. The phrase has become so common that its origins are being forgotten. But it stems from the greatest single mass killing of US citizens outside of natural disasters – wars included. Over 900 people died, and they all wanted to. They were members of the People's Temple, a religious cult presided over by a man whose name lives in infamy – Jim Jones.

Founded by Jones in 1954, the People's Temple of the Disciples of Christ, to give it its full name, was a Christian organization which preached socialism and racial equality – African Americans made up a large number of its adherents. At its height in the late 1970s, the cult had around 5,000 adherents, although the church itself claimed 20,000 followers. It forged strong links with state welfare groups in its home in California, assisting with drug addiction and homelessness programmes. In many ways, it seemed a model of progressive Christianity.

But beneath the façade of religious tolerance and the fight for equality, there were much darker forces at work. Jim Jones was no longer a Christian – to insiders at the church he would, over time, admit to being an atheist who used the Bible to win power. By the 1970s, Jones preached communal living, and his followers were expected to share everything; there was no private property. Children were seen as community assets, and Jones stressed strict physical discipline, enforced by himself or church elders. He now wished to be called "The Prophet" and came under suspicion for relieving his adherents of their income for his own gain.

Jones was born in Indiana in 1931. His father was a veteran of the First World War who suffered from severe breathing difficulties due to injuries that he sustained in a chemical weapons attack. The family was poor, and he lived in a house without electricity and running water. His mother neglected him, and he often wandered the streets of the town, sometimes naked, until other women took him in.

It is said he was obsessed with religion and death, holding mock funerals for roadkill and, rumour had it, killing animals himself. He became fascinated with the Nazi Party during the Second World War, imitating Hitler and the goosestepping of the German army. He would later say that he was ready to kill – he had found no love and only wanted to destroy.

Then, given a Bible by a local pastor, he became a radical adherent of Christianity, often forcing fellow students at school to stop what they were doing so he could read to them from the scriptures, much to their annoyance. He studied at Indiana University, where he was particularly impressed by socialist theories. He then became a Methodist minister before joining a movement called Latter Rain.

It was at a convention in June 1956 that Jones decided – and was told – he had a gift for preaching. His charisma behind and before the pulpit was "supernatural", some said. Other churches were too small and too unambitious for his gift. The People's Temple was born and began to grow.

In 1961, Jones moved the ministry from Indiana to California, having received visions of a nuclear attack on Indianapolis. They later moved to San Francisco. By now there were reports of abuse within the church, sexual, physical and emotional. Jones himself had started taking drugs and was growing increasingly paranoid. He performed faith healing, and his claims were investigated by medical boards that found he was deceiving his followers. He was also arrested for masturbating in a movie theatre, and although the charge was dismissed his paranoia led him to believe the church was about to be raided.

It was then, in 1973, that he took the most dramatic action yet. He decided to move his church out of the US and into Guyana, where he would set up an agricultural commune. The plan took four years, but by early 1977, a thousand of his followers relocated to his "ideal community" – which he named Jonestown. Of these followers, 68 per cent were Black, and Jones was praised for his efforts at racial integration and at forming a "people's utopia".

The reality at the commune was far different. Followers worked eight-hour days of hard labour, followed by eight hours of study of the Bible and socialist tracts. As they worked, they had to listen to Jones on loudspeaker giving orders and reading his theories to them. Mind control and behaviour modification techniques were used. He also subjected his followers to defence drills in case of attack, some of which lasted for six days. The drills included practising "revolutionary suicide", during which all followers would kill themselves rather than be defeated. They practised with unpoisoned drinks.

On 18 November 1978, the commune was visited by US congressman Leo Ryan, who was investigating human rights abuses, and a number of journalists. Ryan was almost stabbed by a follower, and he and his entourage left hurriedly, taking 15 members of the church with them. But at the airstrip, as they prepared to leave, five of the entourage, including Ryan, were shot dead by People's Temple adherents.

Back at the commune, Jones had started preparing for a military attack by the US. His aides laced a large tub of Kool-Aid with a cocktail of drugs, including cyanide. Temple members were told that an attack was imminent. It was time for revolutionary suicide. Each member could drink the Kool-Aid, or it would be injected into them by an elder. A woman named Ruletta Paul and her one-year-old child were the first to consume the poison. As the number of bodies grew, panic spread among some followers, especially those who watched their children die. But witnesses said the majority of the dead had "quietly waited their own turn to die".

In the end, the death toll was 909, with 276 of them being children. Jones was found dead on the stage of the central pavilion; he was resting on a pillow near his deck chair with a gunshot wound to his head. We will never know if it was murder or suicide. But Jim Jones was dead.

SHOKO ASAHARA

It was an attack which spread terror across Japan. The Japanese subway system is one of the engineering wonders of the modern world, carrying nearly 14 million passengers per day on average. Tokyo alone carries around 6 million. So when a chemical attack occurred on the Tokyo subway on 20 March 1995, millions of people feared for their lives. The attack was the brainchild of one man, Shoko Asahara, leader of a doomsday cult known as Aum Shinrikyo.

In fact, it was the second such attack – nine months earlier gas had been released from a converted refrigerator truck in Matsumoto, leading to five deaths and 500 others becoming sick. That had been a trial run by the group. Tokyo was the real thing.

Born Chizuo Matsumoto in 1955, Shoko Asahara had infantile glaucoma from birth, which made him lose all sight in his left eye and go partially blind in his right. The expression "in the land of the blind, the one-eyed man is king" applies to his childhood – sent to a school for the blind, his partial sight enabled him to be a bully, often beating and extorting money from his classmates.

Graduating in 1973, he failed to get into university and established a Chinese medicine shop outside Tokyo. He married – he would father six children – and became interested in religion. From 1984, he visited India a number of times and met the Dalai Lama in Tibet. Returning to Japan in 1987, he now called himself a guru and claimed to be able to levitate during meditation.

At first, his activities seemed innocent enough – he started yoga and meditation classes, and he produced comics and cartoons that used Japanese styles of animation to preach his religious ideas, including both Christianity and Buddhism. Gradually growing more ambitious and surer of his destiny, he began to claim he had healing powers. His sermons of positive thinking – the "Aum salvation plan" – attracted a middle-class following, and he was able to grow his new "religion" financially.

His activities started to generate negative attention. It was claimed he used shock treatment on his followers, kept them against their will and, as he had done at school, extorted money from them. At the same time, he became obsessed with Biblical prophecies and began to regard himself as a prophet. The Aum salvation plan was becoming a cult, and anyone attempting to leave, or anyone who spoke against it, was an enemy.

And enemies should be killed. In October 1989, Tsutsumi Sakamoto, a lawyer working on a class action against Aum, gave a television interview detailing his case. Unbeknown to Sakamoto, the television station foolishly showed the interview to Aum members to get a reaction from them. Their response was swift. On 5 November, five Aum members broke into

Sakamoto's house and beat him and his wife to death, injecting them with potassium chloride to be sure. They did the same to the couple's 14-month-old son. They then stored the bodies in metal drums and placed them in three different locations. Not until after the Tokyo attacks would their bodies be found, completely decomposed.

A number of other critics were also assassinated, including former members. But Shoko Asahara had greater ambitions than just individual deaths. He had begun experimenting with chemicals and managed to manufacture sarin, a colourless, odourless nerve agent which can kill within ten minutes. Those who survive usually suffer permanent neurological damage. Asahara was ready to murder in greater numbers.

The town of Matsumoto had organized a petition of 140,000 signatures – about 70 per cent of the town's population – in an attempt to prevent Aum from setting up an office and factory in the city's southern area. The case had gone to court. Asahara decided to release the gas in the courthouse. When they found out this was locked, he set up a truck outside where the three judges in the case were staying.

On 27 June 1994, 12 litres of liquid sarin were turned into aerosol and pumped into the street. The effect was immediate. Some 274 people were rushed to hospital, suffering from headaches, nausea, diarrhoea, miosis and numbness in their hands. Eight people died, and a nearby lake was found to be full of dead fish. Dogs, birds and trees in the area were also dead. Aum was not suspected.

That changed when the Tokyo subway was gassed. Believing authorities were about to raid Aum's headquarters, Asahara organized an attack. On Monday, 20 March 1995, at rush hour, sarin was released in three locations by operatives dropping packages of the nerve agent and puncturing them with umbrellas. Somewhere between 1,000 and 6,000 commuters were affected, with 13 deaths and 54 suffering serious illness.

Security cameras captured many of the perpetrators, and some themselves suffered poisoning. All roads led back to Shoko Asahara and Aum. The cult's headquarters in Tokyo was raided by police on 16 May 1995. They found stockpiles of chemicals that could be used to produce enough sarin to kill 4 million people. Asahara was arrested and charged with 27 counts of murder. The trial lasted seven years, and he was sentenced to death, as were six fellow cult members. After 14 years of appeals, they were all hanged on 6 July 2018 at Tokyo Detention House. His ashes remain there in order to prevent them from being honoured by former cult members.

THOMAS SILVERSTEIN

It may not technically be a cult, but the Aryan Brotherhood requires absolute discipline from its members. It has one mission, white supremacy, and will stop at nothing to achieve this. And its members are no ordinary men – they are inmates of high-security prisons, each one evil in their own way. So to become leader of the Brotherhood – and to become a man held in solitary confinement for longer than any other inmate in US history – you need to be about as evil as it is possible to be. Thomas Silverstein is that man.

The Brotherhood itself was set up in the 1960s as prisons became desegregated. In 1975, it started a race war among inmates, with Black prisoners being targeted for no other reason than the colour of their skin. By then members of the Brotherhood wore tattoos to show their allegiance, including swastikas, the initials "AB" and the Celtic shamrock, which they took as a symbol of racial purity. They were also made to pledge allegiance to what was called the "blood in, blood out" oath – the only exit from the Aryan Brotherhood was by death.

Thomas Silverstein was in prison for armed robbery. Born in California in 1952, he was a timid and awkward boy, and his divorced mother used to beat him to teach him to stand up to bullies. By 14, he was in a youth correctional facility, and in 1971, at the age of 19, he was jailed for the first time for holding up a bank. Paroled after four years, he did the same thing and this time was sentenced to 15 years.

It was in 1980 that he joined the Aryan Brotherhood. His sentence had already been updated to life after he was charged with killing another inmate, Danny Atwell, who reportedly refused to serve as a mule for heroin being moved through the prison. In 1981, he made his first racially motivated killing, a Black inmate named Robert Chappelle. He and another member of the Brotherhood, Clayton Fountain, strangled Chappelle in his cell.

Not long after, the pair killed again, this time Raymond Smith, a Black friend of Chappelle. Smith was stabbed 67 times. Then they dragged his body up and down the catwalk in front of the cells, displaying it to other prisoners. Silverstein received another two life sentences, one for each of the murders. Given the secretive nature of the Brotherhood – they don't keep paperwork – we don't know exactly whether he was the leader at this point, but he was definitely a very active member.

But Silverstein and Fountain had bigger fish to fry. They hatched a plan to kill a prison guard each, and on 22 October 1983, they did so. Silverstein went first. He had picked his target months earlier, 51-year-old white officer Merle Clutts. As he was being led to the shower block by two other guards, with Clutts walking ahead, Silverstein used an improvised knife to break free of his handcuffs, shook off the other guards and leaped at Clutts. In a frenzy, he stabbed the guard 40 times before he could be dragged off. A few hours later Fountain used exactly the same method to kill another corrections officer, Robert Hoffmann.

The murders were so shocking that the prison itself, United States Penitentiary, Marion, was placed on indefinite lockdown – a lockdown which would, in fact, last 23 years. Prisoners spent most of their time in solitary confinement, seldom seeing anyone else. But more was needed. So grievous were Silverstein and Fountain's actions, and so dangerous were they held to be, that a new type of prison was needed – the supermax, meaning super-maximum security.

In a supermax, prisoners are kept in solitary confinement for 23 hours a day, having minimal contact with staff or other inmates. Communication with others is "minimal to none". Punishment is at the discretion of the guard, without outside review, and there are no systems for prisoners to appeal such punishment. There is little or no access to options for rehabilitation, such as books or education. Meals are passed through ports in the doors. The one hour is for exercise. The first supermax, ADX Florence, was opened in Colorado in 1994, although Silverstein was not sent there immediately.

After the murders, Silverstein had been transferred to USP Atlanta and placed in solitary confinement, his papers marked "no human contact". He was later transferred to USP Leavenworth, where he would spend the next 18 years locked in his cell. Finally, in 2005, he was transferred to the supermax his action had helped bring into being. With his life sentences, his earliest possible date of release was 2 November 2095.

He didn't make it, dying in 2019 aged 67. By then he had been in solitary confinement for 36 years. During those 36 years, it is believed that no prison guard ever spoke to him, in memory of Officer Clutts. Silverstein argued that this long in solitary confinement amounted to a form of torture which violated his legal human rights. But as one prison official put it, "We can't execute Silverstein, so we have no choice but to make his life a living hell. Otherwise, other inmates will kill guards too."

And Clayton Fountain? He converted to Catholicism and completed, via the Catholic Distance University, several educational courses on theology during the 20 years he spent in virtual isolation. He was allowed to correspond with an order of Trappist monks, who posthumously made him a lay brother after his death from a heart attack, aged 48, in 2004.

The Aryan Brotherhood remains active.

JOSEPH KIBWETEERE

There are two big questions which remain unanswered regarding the 778 members of the Movement for the Restoration of the Ten Commandments of God found dead in Uganda. Was this, like the Jonestown Massacre, a mass suicide? Or was it a mass murder? And did their leader, Joseph Kibweteere, and four other cult leaders – Joseph Kasapurari, John Kamagara, Dominic Kataribabo and Credonia Mwerinde – escape? Or are they among the dead?

Mwerinde and Kibweteere were the founders of the cult in 1989. Mwerinde was the daughter of Paolo Kashaku, who claimed to have had visions of his dead daughter, Evangelista, as far back as 1960, and in 1988, he saw visions of Jesus and the Virgin Mary. In 1989, Mwerinde, then 27 and working as a prostitute, claimed to have also had a vision of Mary.

Later that year she met Joseph Kibweteere, who had been having similar visions. Born in 1932, he came from a wealthy Catholic family, and back in 1980, he had run for office.

Married in 1960, he had spent the last few years before he met Mwerinde spreading the gospel of his visions.

The pair formed the Movement for the Restoration of the Ten Commandments of God, usually known as the MRTC. Their encounters with the Virgin had convinced them that the apocalypse was coming, and they co-authored a book called *A Timely Message from Heaven: The End of the Present Time*. It won the church a substantial following of around 1,000 acolytes. As head of the church, Kibweteere appointed 12 apostles, six men and six women, and set dates for when the apocalypse would come.

These dates passed without incident.

Another vision told Kibweteere that the year 2000 would be followed by Year 1 of the new world. The followers of MRTC would be saved, and all others damned.

On 17 March, the Movement, believing that the end of the world was nigh, held a giant party at their church building. They roasted three bulls and drank 70 crates of Coca-Cola they had purchased. It was later revealed that several days earlier, Movement leader Dominic Kataribabo was seen buying 50 litres of sulfuric acid.

It was late in the afternoon that villagers heard a giant explosion. Rushing to the church, they found it engulfed in flames – some said it had been boarded up to stop anyone leaving. Some 530 bodies were later found, charred beyond recognition.

Police immediately descended on the cult's other compounds. In one they found 153 bodies, and in another 155. The majority had been poisoned or stabbed. At a farm belonging to one of Kibweteere's apostles, another 81 bodies were found. Finally, in the latrine back at Kanungu, six bodies were found, locked in and left to starve.

Was this suicide, or was it murder? And did Kibweteere perish or escape? According to the police, this was murder – on realizing that his prophecy for the end of the world was doomed once again to fail, Kibweteere decided to slaughter his followers. The vice president of Uganda said, "These were... well-orchestrated mass murders perpetrated by a network of diabolic, malevolent criminals masquerading as religious people." Diabolic and malevolent – meaning evil.

An international arrest warrant exists for Kibweteere's arrest. If captured, he would be tried for mass murder on a scale that almost defies belief.

WARREN JEFFS

In 1879, the United States Supreme Court passed a law outlawing polygamy – the act of taking multiple husbands or wives, which generally meant wives – in the US. This left the state of Utah with a problem – its main church, the Church of Jesus of the Latter-day Saints, commonly known as the Mormon Church, had always practised polygamy. Utah was informed it could not join the Union unless the practice was banned in accordance with federal law.

Eleven years later, after much debate, church president Wilford Woodruff issued the "1890 Manifesto", which ended the practice, although those already married were able to stay so. And in 1896, Utah was able to join the Union.

Not everyone was happy. Various splinter groups left the main church and set up their own sects. One such sect was the Fundamentalist Church of Jesus Christ of Latter-Day Saints (FLDS), which was set up in Short Creek, Arizona. It was always under the eye of authorities, and a raid in 1953 saw the greatest arrest of polygamists in history. Some 236 children were taken from their parents; 150 of them were not returned. The church continued, though, staying mostly under the radar of law enforcement. That changed in 2006 when its leader was placed on the FBI's Ten Most Wanted Fugitives list. His name was Warren Jeffs, and he was wanted for child abuse.

Born to FLDS parents – his father, Rulon Jeffs, became president of the church in 1986 and had, it is believed, 65 wives, producing 65 children during his lifetime – Warren was brought up in the church. When his father died at the age of 92 in 2002, Jeffs replaced him as president.

He also replaced him as a husband – Jeffs immediately married all but two of his father's wives. One refused, and the other fled the church. Of those he married, a number are believed to have been underage.

Soon after, he expelled a number of rivals for power in the church – excommunicating them and "reassigning" their wives to himself and others. By now the police were becoming interested again in the activities of the Short Creek Community. Then, in July 2005, all hell broke loose.

A nephew of Jeffs, Brent, filed suit accusing three of his uncles, including Warren Jeffs, of sexually assaulting him when he was only five years old. This was no single incident but, he claimed, a regular occurrence in the community. He held that children were subjected to sexual abuse on a systematic basis, and Jeffs was an active participant.

Details began to emerge of the ways in which Jeffs ran the community. Television, movies, popular music and fictional books were banned, while rules of behaviour were strictly enforced. Women were told to "keep sweet" by suppressing their emotions and feelings and obeying their husbands. In particular, they were to obey Jeffs. Jeffs continued to perform marriages, often between girls under 18 and older men. He continued to take more wives, many of them also underage.

In June 2005, Jeffs was charged with sexual assault on a minor and conspiracy to commit sexual misconduct with a minor after arranging a marriage between a then-14-year-old girl and her 19-year-old first cousin, Allen Steed. The girl, Elissa Wall, later wrote a book about her experiences, including rapes and miscarriages.

Facing an increasing number of charges as more and more evidence of forced child-bride marriages emerged, Jeffs fled, hiding out in various cities around the US. Utah issued an arrest warrant for him on felony charges of accomplice rape of a teenage girl between 14 and 18 years old. He also made the FBI's Ten Most Wanted Fugitives list, with a reward of $100,000 offered. On 27 May 2008, The Smoking Gun website released images of Jeffs with two underage wives, one of whom was 12 years old, celebrating their first wedding anniversaries in 2005 and 2006.

In August 2006, the law finally caught up with Jeffs. He was arrested in Nevada and returned by police to Utah. His trial began on 11 September 2007, and he was found guilty on two counts of being an accomplice to rape. He was sentenced to ten years in jail.

He also faced charges in Texas, two counts of sexual assault of a child. A raid by authorities had found horrific evidence incriminating Jeffs – including an audio recording of him having sexual relations with a 12-year-old. Officials also discovered a pregnant 15-year-old at the ranch who was carrying Jeffs' child. He was found guilty and sentenced to life in prison, with the first possibility of parole in 2038.

In prison, he has engaged in hunger strikes and predicted doomsday a number of times. Some members of the church still see him as their leader. But others have continued to come forward with stories of abuse – there are crimes that Jeffs has not answered for, and it seems unlikely he will ever be released.

JOSEPH DI MAMBRO

The baby was two months old and named Christopher-Emmanuel. On 30 September 1994, his parents, Antonio Dutoit and Suzanne Robinson, members of the Order of the Solar Temple (OST), were lured to the Quebec chalet of the cult's founder and leader, Joseph di Mambro. There they were met by another couple, Colette and Gerry Genoud, also members of the OST. As soon as they arrived with their baby, the Genouds attacked them, stabbing them to death. They then took the baby and drove a stake through his heart.

Three days later, having flown to Zurich, the Genouds committed suicide on the orders of their leader. Joseph di Mambro wanted no loose ends in the killing of what he regarded as the Antichrist. It was not the first, or the last, of his evil crimes.

Di Mambro's belief that Christopher-Emmanuel was the Antichrist was based on two things. First, the pair had not asked his permission to conceive – a fundamental rule in his sect. Second, the child shared part of its name with his own daughter, Emmanuelle – who he had brought up in the belief that she was a cosmic child, born to save the universe. He believed her to be the reincarnation of the gods and prophets Osiris, Akhenaten and Moses, and the Italian occultist Cagliostro. By usurping her name, the baby had threatened the whole cosmic order.

Joseph di Mambro was born in Pont-Saint-Esprit, France, in 1924. When he was still a child his sister had been decapitated when she stuck her head out of a train window. Di Mambro would often tell this story with undisguised glee.

He was apprenticed as a jeweller and watchmaker at 16. At the end of the Second World War the French economy collapsed, and di Mambro sought other work. Always interested in the esoteric, he decided to become a medium and soon regarded himself as the reincarnation of a "great spirit" from the past. He was also a thief, forced to flee Pont-Saint-Esprit after stealing gold and silver from a local jeweller.

Returning to Pont-Saint-Esprit in 1972, he was soon jailed for six months for fraud and impersonating a psychiatrist. In jail he approached members of the Sovereign Military Order of the Temple of Jerusalem, a white supremacist Templar order, and may have joined them. On his release in 1973, he went deeper into occult groups, and over the next ten years he moved around various esoteric organizations.

It was in 1981 that he met Luc Jouret, who gave a lecture about links between the occult and homeopathy. The pair became close friends, and in 1984, they founded the OST. Jouret would be the face of the organization. But it was di Mambro, working behind the scenes, who was the true leader.

One of the things he organized was the birth of the cosmic child, Emmanuelle. The child would, said di Mambro, be conceived by theogamy – the marriage of a mortal and a god. The mortal would be 19-year-old cult member Dominique Bellaton, a prostitute and drug addict who had joined the order at the urging of her parents.

A ceremony was performed without sexual intercourse, and Bellaton appeared to fall pregnant soon after. It later transpired that di Mambro and Bellaton had been having an affair, and she was already several weeks pregnant when the ceremony took place. But Emmanuelle was received as a god when she was born on 21 March 1982. She was forced to protect her purity as a child by wearing gloves and a helmet.

Twelve years later Christopher-Emmanuel received a stake through his heart.

By then membership numbers had started falling, as evidence that many of the esoteric happenings at services, such as apparitions appearing, had been faked. But a number of members stayed with the group, di Mambro manipulating them with fear of punishment and even death. He referred to his followers as "weak souls".

But Emmanuelle was starting to rebel and preferred the company of other children to being a cosseted cosmic child. In 1993, Jouret had been arrested for purchasing illegal weapons. And di Mambro, unbeknown to his followers, had developed cancer – his kidneys were failing, and he was incontinent. Four days after the murder of Christopher-Emmanuel, followers were summoned to two locations in Switzerland, Cheiry and Salvan. Fires broke out at both shortly before midnight on 4 October. The fire department found 23 people dead in Cheiry and 25 in Salvan.

The dead included di Mambro and Bellaton. Luc Jouret was also dead. It was determined at the inquest that the majority who died were given tranquilizers and were subsequently shot. The victims were, in most cases, "dressed in a white, black or gold ritual cloak, depending on the degree of initiation reached". Their bodies were arranged in a circular pattern, and they had plastic bags on their heads. The Swiss magistrate concluded that of the deaths, only 15 were actual suicides.

Horrifyingly, at least five of the dead were children, including the cosmic child, Emmanuelle.

DANIEL PEREZ

He was, he said, an angel, and he could predict the exact moment you were going to die. But he could also make sure you returned from the dead. All you had to do was make your life insurance out to him. That Daniel Perez – who called himself Lou Castro – was able to convince so many people to do this for him shows how charismatic he was. That he tried to do it to others shows how evil he was too.

He named his cult, and its location, Angel's Landing, a vast 20-acre plot on the northern outskirts of Wichita, Kansas. There, posing as a wise man, he lured vulnerable victims with promises of divine insight and his ability to perform miracles. He also claimed to be able to cure diseases.

Members of the cult came from all over the US. Arriving at Angel's Landing, they would be persuaded to submit to his powers, and if they were sick, Perez promised to restore them to health. He was seen as innocent and caring. A true angel. But he had one particular problem, he told them. He was centuries old, and that meant his powers could wane – he might even die. He needed, he told them, to have sex with young girls to stay alive. They had to be between eight and 16 years old.

One woman later told of how her family had joined the commune when she was young. Her mother was terrified that Perez would die. And so she offered up her daughter to be raped. This happened on a regular basis to many of the girls at Angel's Landing. "I was 10 when my childhood was over," one girl later said. "While other 10-year-olds were riding bikes or playing with dolls, I was laying naked in a bed with a pillow over my head, just waiting for it to be over." He told the girls he was "fixing" them.

Meanwhile, a number of followers died mysterious deaths or just went missing. Many had signed over their life insurance to Perez – who, despite having no employment history, grew very wealthy. Over the course of seven years, he collected millions of dollars in life insurance payouts.

In fact, it was an attempt to open a bank account in a false name in 2010 that saw him finally arrested, facing 28 charges, including rape, aggravated criminal sodomy, sexual exploitation of a child, and aggravated assault with a deadly weapon and murder. In February 2015, aged 55 – the centuries-old angel had, in fact, been born in Texas in 1959 – he was convicted on all counts and sentenced to 80 years in jail, with no possibility of parole.

The angel had finally fallen to Earth.

STEVEN TARI

He called himself the Black Jesus, and he claimed religious affiliation with the Christian tradition, even seeing himself as the New Messiah. But when Steven Tari was hacked to death and castrated by angry villagers seeking vengeance for his crimes, there was no resurrection, and certainly no one wept.

And what were the crimes? There were probably more than we will ever know of, but those we do know are shocking and sickening. He was a murderer. He was a cannibal. But the most notorious of his crimes was his use of "flower girls" who served as his concubines – and they were indeed girls, all of them underage, and all of them raped by Tari on a regular basis.

He was born on Manus Island in Papua New Guinea in 1971 and studied to become a Lutheran minister. But during his studies he had a revelation and came to reject the Bible. Dropping out, he retreated into the mountain village of Gal, taking with him no possessions, not even clothes. There he announced himself as the new Messiah and began to gather followers, using his charisma to draw in those who felt lost. These followers would number 6,000, and they included the flower girls he would use for his pleasure.

One was Rita Harman. Her mother, Barmarhal, had joined the cult when her daughter was 13 and was soon regarded as the queen of the flower girls. Her daughter was offered up to Tari in exchange for gifts of material goods and wealth, as well as spiritual rewards in this and the next life. Tari took the girl to his tent and raped her repeatedly. He then stabbed her multiple times, killing her. It is not known if he ate her flesh, but rumours persist.

This was to set a pattern for all that followed. Young girls would be brought to Tari, raped and then killed. Tari insisted they be virgins, and it is rumoured some were as young as eight. We can never know how many girls he assaulted and killed, but he claimed to have had sex with over 430 flower girls. He regarded each of his victims as being married to him and told their parents that the girls would meet them again in heaven.

Sexual assault wasn't his only crime – he and his followers forced schools and churches in the area to close down, stole or burned crops, and burned down the homes of villagers who didn't follow the cult. When a Lutheran minister, Logan Sapus, was sent by authorities to infiltrate the cult, he ended up joining and later helped Tari escape after his first arrest in 2005.

It was in 2007 that he was finally arrested and charged – he had been hunted by rival villagers to a place called Matepi in Madang Province. The villagers called the police, and after a brief shootout, Tari was arrested. He was charged with sexual offences only – there was no hard proof of the murders as the bodies were gone, and no parent would press charges. The trial lasted three years, during which Tari was incarcerated – he tried to escape on numerous occasions. He was found guilty of four rapes and sentenced to 20 years in prison.

But on 21 March 2013, Tari was one of 48 prisoners who effected a mass breakout from Beon Prison Camp. He took refuge in the village of Gal, with locals helping to hide him.

However, he could not stay straight for long – on 31 August, he organized the ritualistic rape and murder of a 15-year-old schoolgirl, Rose Wagum, who was taken to his camp by her aunt, and then he attempted the same with a 14-year-old the next day.

Hearing of the assaults, a posse of 80 Gal men descended on Tari the next day. They tied a rope around his neck and dragged him to a remote spot outside the village. An autopsy would reveal that "he was chopped and slashed with bush knives on both arms and legs, chest and stomach, which revealed his intestines. He was also castrated." His body was then buried in a shallow pit.

No one was ever charged with his murder, and the district administrator, Lawrence Pitor, was blunt about why not. He said: "Those who live by the sword die by the sword. [Tari] brought his own demise by the evil he dwelled in."

DAVID KORESH

At approximately 9.30 a.m. on 28 February 1993, the Federal Bureau of Alcohol, Tobacco, Firearms and Explosives (ATF) approached a compound at the Mount Carmel Center in Waco, Texas. They had organized a search warrant after receiving information that the religious sect using the centre, the Branch Davidians, had been stockpiling weapons. They also had an arrest warrant for the leader of the sect, a man named David Koresh, and some of his followers.

Unbeknown to them, the Branch Davidians had received a tip-off – a journalist had asked the local postmaster where Mount Carmel was. The postmaster was the brother-in-law of Koresh. So when the ATF approached the building, the Branch Davidians were prepared. And they started firing.

Over the next two hours, four agents were killed and 16 injured. Inside the compound five Branch Davidians were shot dead, three outright, and two killed by fellow Branch Davidians after having been wounded. A number of sect members were also wounded, including Koresh.

With the agents running out of ammunition, a ceasefire was called, and the Branch Davidians allowed the ATF to evacuate its dead and wounded. A later inquest would argue that the sect had not maximized the number of agents it killed during the firing. After all, what is the point of killing people when you are expecting the end of the world?

The Branch Davidians had been formed in 1955 by Benjamin Roden as an offshoot of the Seventh-Day Adventists and were a doomsday cult, believing the end of the world was nigh. They purchased Mount Carmel in 1962 and the lands around it in 1973. Benjamin's death in 1978 saw his wife Lois become leader of the church.

In 1981, she started teaching a young man named Vernon Howell. Born in 1959, he had been brought up by his grandmother, who he believed to be his mother. Shortly after the truth was revealed, he was sexually abused by one of his real mother's male relatives. At 19, he had an illegal sexual relationship with a 16-year-old girl, who became pregnant and ran away, never to be seen again. Obsessed with sex, he then had a relationship with another 15-year-old, his pastor's daughter. Forced to flee, he ended up at Mount Carmel and studied under Lois.

By 1983, Howell, who was now starting to call himself David Koresh (Koresh being a translation of Cyrus, a Persian king who was named a messiah for freeing Jews during the Babylonian captivity), was claiming the gift of prophecy. He was also, it is believed, having an affair with Lois, then in her sixties. Koresh eventually began to claim that God had chosen him to father a child by Lois, who would be the Chosen One. This did not go down well with George, the son of Benjamin and Lois, and he expelled Koresh from the sect, along with some members who had begun following him.

When Lois died, the splinter group under Koresh returned to Mount Carmel and shot George Roden. He survived but was later jailed for the murder of a fellow member, Wayman Dale Adair, whom Roden claimed Koresh had sent to kill him. In 1989, Koresh became the leader of the Branch Davidians.

Accusations of physical and sexual abuse of children followed Koresh. He believed that he had to have 24 children who would oversee the coming of Christ, and he engaged in polygamy, taking multiple wives, some as young as 15. Allegations were made that he had fathered offspring with underage girls in the Branch Davidians and had been seen beating children. This, coupled with the weapon allegations, led the ATF to obtain warrants for the raid.

After the ceasefire, the FBI was brought in. They would institute a siege that would last 51 days and grip the world. Koresh, who had been badly wounded, gave multiple press interviews, while bombarding FBI negotiators with Biblical quotations and prophesizing the end of the world. His cause was taken up by various civil liberty groups and gun owner associations, with supporters gathering outside the compound – including Timothy McVeigh, who would later carry out the Oklahoma City bombing.

The FBI treated it as a hostage situation; those held included 23 children, 14 of whom had been fathered by Koresh. Negotiation was initially seen as offering the best chance of ending the siege, but FBI tactics became increasingly aggressive. Electricity and water were cut off.

By now Koresh was claiming to be the Second Coming of Christ and that the Book of Revelations was coming true – the Davidians would only leave once it was fulfilled. It was believed by agents that children continued to be abused within the compound. The very fact that Koresh would not release the children shows the evil that lurked within him, whether they were being assaulted or not.

US Attorney General Janet Reno sought the support of President Bill Clinton to attack the compound. The assault took place at dawn on 19 April 1993. The FBI, with orders not to shoot, even if shot at, released tear gas into the compound. Shots rang out from inside. But after six hours of increasing levels of harassment, no Branch Davidians had left. It appeared the attack had failed.

Then, around noon, three fires broke out. The government blamed the Branch Davidians; surviving Branch Davidians blamed the FBI. Nine people managed to escape – the other 76 died inside, including all the children. Koresh was shot by his deputy, Steve Schneider, who then shot himself.

Autopsy records also indicate that as well as Koresh, at least 20 Branch Davidians were shot, as well as five children under the age of 14. A three-year-old had been stabbed in the chest. The Branch Davidians claimed these were mercy killings; the FBI called them executions.

Koresh is buried at Memorial Park Cemetery in Tyler, Texas. The apocalypse has not occurred.

ADOLFO CONSTANZO

They were called the Narcosatanists, and he was known as El Padrino, The Godfather. They were drug traffickers in Mexico, but that was the least of their crimes. The Narcosatanists specialized in ritual murders, but only after they had tortured their victims. Their mix of occultism and narcotics would terrify Mexico throughout the 1980s. And their leader, Adolfo Constanzo, continues to inspire fear, even after his death in 1989.

He was born in 1962 in Miami, Florida, to Delia Aurora González, a Cuban immigrant. He was immediately attracted to religion, serving as an altar boy but also dabbling in voodoo. He also started practising magic and following a Cuban religion called Palo Mayombe, which includes animal sacrifice – like so many of those who become serial killers, torturing and killing animals was part of his childhood. He and his mother were arrested several times for theft and vandalism.

In 1983, he pledged himself to Kadiempembe, the Palo Mayombe equivalent of the Devil, and moved to Mexico

City, meeting three men who would become his followers: Martín Quintana, Jorge Montes and Omar Orea Ochoa. He also began a sexual relationship with both Quintana and Ochoa. They began to run a profitable business casting spells to bring good luck, mostly to wealthy drug dealers. The spells involved animal sacrifice, and the more the client paid, the rarer the animal – from chickens to goats, zebras and even lion cubs.

Constanzo had also started raiding graveyards for human bones to use in his spells. But it was almost inevitable that he would later decide the bones of the dead were not enough. He needed live human sacrifices to make his spells more powerful, and he told his followers that he needed them to die in pain.

In the murky underworld of Mexico and its drug dealers in the 1980s, it is hard to be certain how many victims suffered at the hands of Constanzo and his group, now calling themselves the Narcosatanists. We do know that 20 mutilated bodies were found around Mexico City – the Narcosatanists would torture their victims before killing them in order to increase the power of the spells, and the bodies showed signs of ritual abuse.

As the cartels that Constanzo blessed kept increasing their profits, their magician wanted a bigger slice of the pie. He approached the powerful Calzadas family and demanded to be made a full business partner in return for his support. They refused. Soon after, seven Calzadas family members went missing. When their bodies were found, they had been mutilated beyond recognition. They were missing ears, toes, fingers, even brains. One was missing his spine.

Constanzo now approached the powerful Hernandez family with the same offer. They agreed.

Sometime soon after, he met Sara Aldrete, who he would appoint as his second-in-command. La Madrina (The Godmother) to his El Padrino. She became an enthusiastic comrade, often helping Constanzo carry out the sacrifices, as well as helping him in his drug dealing. Together they set up a new headquarters at Rancho Santa Elena, where they could store drugs and bodies.

Up until 1989, their victims were prostitutes, homeless persons or drug dealers, and the police did little to follow up on the crimes. That changed on 14 March 1989. The previous day, the group had sacrificed and killed a stranger to ensure the safe passage of a shipment of 800 kilos of marijuana Constanzo was trading. He didn't feel it was enough. With a shipment so big, he needed to up the ante. He wanted an American, and he wanted their brain.

Mark J. Kilroy was a Texan pre-med student who was in Mexico on spring break. The group abducted him from outside a bar and took him back to the ranch. There he was tortured before they split his head open with a machete. Another victim of the Narcosatanists.

But unlike the others, his disappearance was noted. Kilroy was part of a wealthy family, who demanded an investigation. Texan police pressured their Mexico City compatriots. Following various leads, the police descended on Rancho Santa Elena. There they found 15 bodies, all mutilated, including that of Kilroy. They also searched Constanzo's home and found a torture chamber. Constanzo was not there.

But his luck had run out. Police were going door to door, carrying out an unrelated search for a missing child near where Constanzo and three of his followers, Aldrete, Quintana and Alvaro De Leon, were hiding. Seeing the police approach,

Constanzo opened fire. Reinforcements were called – 180 officers rushed to the scene.

Knowing he was defeated and not wanting to face prison, Constanzo ordered De Leon to shoot him as well as Martin Quintana. De Leon and Aldrete were arrested and charged with murder, drug trafficking and obstructing justice, each receiving long jail sentences. No one was charged with the murder of Kilroy, although his family has promised to press charges if any of the cult members are released.

The body of Constanzo was burned to make sure no one would ever worship at the grave of the evil leader of the Narcosatanists.

JEFFREY LUNDGREN

Sometimes it is not the quantity of the killings that reveals the force of the evil. Cult leader Jeffrey Lundgren did not rack up the body count of many of the men in this book. In fact, he killed only five people, all from one family, and all in one night. But the murders were so cold-blooded that no one can doubt the malevolence that dwelled inside him.

Lundgren was born in Independence, Missouri, in 1950, and he grew up as a member of the Reorganized Church of Jesus Christ of Latter-Day Saints (RLDS). Subject to extreme physical abuse by his father as a child, as a teenager he became an expert in firearms. When he moved to university, he took up residence in a house specially built for fellow RLDS students. There he met Alice Keeler, who had also suffered childhood abuse. The pair married in 1970. After a brief stint in the Navy, he served as a lay minister for the church.

However, financial troubles started to bring out his anger. He and Keeler had four children, and Lundgren struggled to stay afloat. He began beating his wife – she was hospitalized with a ruptured spleen after one physical altercation.

The family moved to Kirtland, Ohio, where he became a guide at the Kirtland Temple, the oldest Latter-Day Saints temple in existence. The position was unpaid, but he began embezzling money from the temple's bookstore, an estimated $40,000 over the next few years. Caught in 1987, he was forced to leave the church. But he had already set up his own one.

The RLDS had become more liberal during the 1980s, allowing female pastors and adopting a stance of inclusivity for LGBT members. Conservative members of the church railed against these stances, and some left and started following Lundgren. He had rented a large farmhouse and set up a community – the adherents called him "Dad". They kept their place in the community by turning their paycheques over to Dad.

Among those who followed him, one family stood out – the Avery family. Unlike the other seven followers, they chose not to live in the community but to stay in their own homes. Lundgren disliked 49-year-old Dennis Avery and thought his wife, 46-year-old Cheryl, was too independent for a woman. He also regarded their three daughters, Trina, 15, Rebecca, 13, and seven-year-old Karen, as too disobedient. And, despite being the biggest financial contributors to Lundgren, they kept a small amount of money for themselves, which Lundgren regarded as a sin.

By now Lundgren was declaring himself a prophet. The world would end soon, and men should prepare themselves with firearms training. The group also needed to reclaim the Kirtland Temple from the liberal arm of the RLDS before Lundgren's 38th birthday in May 1988, and they would do so by force. But this plan was abandoned after a disaffected member went to the police.

Lundgren was angry and told his followers that he had received spiritual guidance that if they wanted to see God, they would have to commit murder. Conveniently, the murder had to be a family of five. It was time, he told his followers, to prune the vineyard. The Averys had to die.

On 10 April 1989, he ordered two of his followers to dig a pit inside the main barn for the bodies. A week later he gathered together his male followers and had them pledge their loyalty to his plan. They did. He then sent one of his followers off to get the Averys. He took them into his house and then asked them one by one to come with him on a special assignment, Dennis first.

Dennis Avery was led to the barn. On the way an attempt to knock him unconscious with a stun gun failed, and he had to be dragged to where Lundgren was waiting for him. He was bound, gagged and shot twice in the back, dying instantly and being thrown into the pit.

To mask the sound of the gun, a chainsaw was left running. It was still running when Cheryl was brought in and met the same fate. Then, one at a time, the three girls were brought in and shot and then thrown in the pit. Last to die was six-year-old Karen Avery, shot in the chest and head.

Purely by coincidence, Kirtland police officers and members of the FBI converged on Lundgren's farm the day after the Avery murders in response to complaints from neighbours about cult activities and improper use of firearms. The officers searched the barn for weapons, unaware they were walking over the graves of the Avery family. No guns were found.

Lundgren and his family fled soon after, first moving to a campsite in West Virginia and later making their way to

Missouri. But he had left behind disgruntled followers. One, Keith Johnson, was especially angry. Lundgren had informed him he had to give up his wife in order for her to marry him, Lundgren, in the polygamist tradition. On 3 January 1990, Johnson went to the police with a map of where the Averys were buried.

The manhunt was brief – by 7 January 1990, Lundgren was behind bars. Thirteen other sect members were also arrested, including Lundgren's wife, Alice, and son, Damon. Alice received five life sentences, and Damon 120 years in prison. Other followers were sentenced to between 20 and 50 years.

Jeffrey Lundgren was sentenced to death. The prosecutor said later, "We kept waiting for the insanity defence, but it never came." Lundgren assured the court he was sane and that he was unrepentant.

He was executed on 24 October 2006. As nobody claimed his body, he was buried on prison grounds.

ROCH THÉRIAULT

He called them the Ant Hill Kids because when he had made them build the cult's compound by hand, they reminded him of ants making an ant hill. Members wore identical tunics and were not allowed to speak to each other. Anyone who tried to leave was beaten, hung from the ceiling or had their body hair plucked out. Sometimes he would even defecate on them and leave them like that until they repented. This was no medieval horror show. This was Québec in the late twentieth century. And he was Roch Thériault.

Born in 1947, he was an intelligent child, but he left school to pursue his religious impulses, from Catholicism to Seventh-Day Adventism, and eventually his own religion. Believing that the end of the world was nigh, he convinced a number of people to sell their belongings, sever ties with their families, and move to where they would live in unity and equality and be free of sin.

But things quickly grew darker.

Now calling himself Moïse, meaning Moses – he also gave all of his followers new Biblical names – Thériault predicted the world would end in February 1979. In preparation, he moved his commune by hiking to a mountainside he called "Eternal Mountain" in Hope, in the sparsely populated Gaspé Peninsula of Canada, where they built their new commune. He set about expanding the group, not by recruiting new members, but by impregnating the women in the sect, fathering over 20 children with nine female members of the group.

The apocalypse failed to come – he argued that time on Earth and in God's world were not parallel, and therefore it was a miscalculation. But that did not loosen his grip on his followers. By now he was drinking heavily, and his control of them became more and more severe. As well as not allowing his followers to speak to each other, he started punishing them for any errors in more and more horrifying ways.

Some he made sit on stoves until they suffered severe burns. He would make others eat dead mice or excrement. Some he made break their own legs with sledgehammers. They were also encouraged to hurt each other – forced to shoot one another in the shoulder or, in a test of loyalty, cut off the toes of another follower. Such was his hold on them that they submitted and tried to do better.

And it wasn't just the adults he attacked. Sexual abuse of the children by Thériault was commonplace, including his own children. Or they were nailed to trees while other children threw stones at them, or they might be held over a fire by an adult until they were dropped. Both children and adults were also subjected to purification through pain – they would be tied naked and whipped.

He also, believing himself to be a holy man with curing powers, decided to carry out surgical operations on sect members, injecting a 94 per cent ethanol solution into their stomachs or performing circumcisions on the children and adults of the group.

It was in 1989 that the abuse became murder, and it did so in the most horrifying way possible. Cult member Solange Boilard complained of an upset stomach. Thériault forced her to undress, laid her on the kitchen table and punched her repeatedly in the stomach. Then he performed an enema by shoving a tube up her rectum and filling her with olive oil. After that he cut her open, ripped out part of her intestines and forced another member to stitch her up. Boilard died, but Thériault believed he could resurrect her by drilling a hole in her head for male members to ejaculate in. It didn't work.

He also killed one of his children in a botched circumcision and another by leaving them outside in a blizzard.

It was not until his final attack, on Gabrielle Lavallée, that he was stopped. During her time in the commune, he burned her genitals with a blowtorch, removed eight of her teeth with pliers and nailed her hand to a table in order to amputate her arm with a hunting knife. He also cut off part of her breasts and struck her head with the blunt edge of an axe. In 1989, after the amputation, Lavallée finally fled and contacted the authorities.

Thériault was arrested and charged with assault for the amputation, receiving 12 years in prison. In 1993, he pleaded guilty to second-degree murder for the death of Solange Boilard and was sentenced to life imprisonment in Dorchester Penitentiary.

On 26 February 2011, Thériault's cellmate Matthew Gerrard MacDonald, a 60-year-old convicted murderer, walked up to the guard's station with a knife dripping in blood. "Here's the knife," he told the guard, "I've sliced him up." Sixty-three-year-old Roch Thériault had been stabbed in the neck, an evil and violent end for an evil and violent man.

FAIZRAKHMAN SATAROV

In August 2011, Russian police were investigating what they described as a terrorist attack that killed a top cleric in oil-rich Tatarstan, a central Russian province where the population is about 60 per cent Muslim. They were aware that one particular sect, with about 70 members, had lived in the area since the 1970s, under the leadership of Faizrakhman Satarov, sharing his three-storey home. The police decided to question the sect as to any involvement, a routine part of the procedure. What they discovered shocked them to the core.

Satarov had been a mufti – an Islamic scholar of law – until the 1960s, when he had a strange vision. A trolleybus was passing him, and the electric cables threw off sparks, a not-unusual occurrence. However, Satarov didn't see just any sparks; he saw the Divine Light of God. He believed himself to have been sent this as a sign that he was a prophet. As Islam recognizes only one prophet, Mohammed, he was excommunicated, and he decided to set up his own sect.

Satarov's house became a school for followers, and their leader adapted Islamic texts such as the Koran to match his visions. Rejecting both Islamic and Russian law, Satarov led his followers into isolation from mainstream society, pursuing religious separatism at its most extreme. The sect, whose members called themselves *muammin* – Arabic for "believers" – had thousands of followers in the 1990s, but they had gradually drifted away from their leader as Satarov's visions became more extreme and his rejection of Islam more total.

What no one outside the sect knew was that one of his visions had given him a mission. The surface of the Earth should no longer be the chosen dwelling place of humanity. His mission was to build an Islamic caliphate underground.

Hearing noises beneath the floor at Satarov's house, the police decided to investigate. To their astonishment, they found beneath the house an eight-level complex of underground chambers, with rooms dug out like catacombs. But that was not the greatest shock.

Living underground were 38 adults and 27 children. And the children, it transpired, had lived their entire lives below ground, never having been allowed to the surface of the Earth. Of the 27 children, aged between one and 17, many were suffering from anaemia, and there were also cases of tuberculosis. They were living, prosecutors said, in conditions not fit for humans.

Neighbours told police that Satarov's sect regarded themselves as the chosen ones and often hurled abuse, and even stones, at those around them. The neighbours also saw the occasional child, who was invariably dirty and appeared malnourished. These children, too, were encouraged to throw stones.

Satarov was charged with negligence and child abuse, as were a number of his followers. He received a five-year jail sentence but was not taken in to serve it as he was suffering from delirium. He died in 2015, and his house was demolished, his manuscripts destroyed. Those remaining at the compound were forced to leave, and his sect disappeared from the face of the Earth.

MARSHALL APPLEWHITE

On 26 March 1997, deputies of the San Diego County Sheriff's Office entered a mansion known as The Monastery in the suburb of Rancho Santa Fe. There they found 39 people – 21 women and 18 men – all dressed identically in black shirts and sweatpants, brand new black-and-white athletic shoes and armband patches reading "Heaven's Gate Away Team". They were all dead.

They were members of the religious cult Heaven's Gate, and their deaths made headlines around the world. These 39 individuals had, they believed, been transported from Earth by a "spaceship". They were off on a journey that their founder, Marshall Applewhite – known to his followers as Do – had predicted for a very long time.

Applewhite had been born in Texas in 1931, the son of a Presbyterian minister. He was very religious as a child. After graduating from school, he earned a bachelor's degree in philosophy in 1952 and subsequently enrolled at Union Presbyterian Seminary to study theology, hoping to become a minister. He married, had two children, served in the army for two years and then enrolled at the University of Colorado, where he earned a master's degree in music. He then started teaching at the University of Alabama. Things seemed to be going swimmingly.

But in 1965, he was fired for pursuing a sexual relationship with a male student. His wife divorced him. He taught for a time at the University of St Thomas in Texas, but again his sexual orientation saw him lose his position. He suffered from depression and found himself in severe financial difficulties.

It was then, in 1972, that he met a woman who would change his life. Bonnie Nettles was a nurse with an interest in Biblical prophecy and theosophy. She told Applewhite that their meeting had been foretold by extraterrestrials, as they had been close in a past life. They were, both knew, soulmates in a non-sexual way. Nettles left her husband and four children, and the pair moved in together, opened a bookshop and started teaching mystic practices.

Growing restless, they began travelling around the US, spreading their message and immersing themselves in the Bible, psychological texts and science fiction. They believed that they were higher minds and that Applewhite may be a new Jesus. They also believed they may be killed, then come back to life and be transported to the heavens in a spaceship. This event would be called The Demonstration and would prove their divine mission.

Gradually they started to gain followers, and by 1975, they had 70 devotees. Following the injunction of Jesus to let go of earthly things, they encouraged their adherents to forsake family, friends, drugs, alcohol, jewellery, the media, facial hair and even sexuality. Applewhite and Nettles now called themselves "Do" and "Ti", and they split their followers into small groups called "Star Clusters". The pair gradually took control of more and more aspects of their followers' lives.

Then, in 1983, Nettles was diagnosed with cancer. Despite her medical background, she refused treatment, believing that she and Applewhite could not die. But they could, and she did, passing away in 1985. Applewhite was devastated and had a crisis of faith. He would later claim that it was his followers who saved him, and he organized a ceremony in which he symbolically married them.

Nettles' death also convinced Applewhite that the body was just a vessel. He and his followers would leave their bodies behind when it came to moving to a new plane of consciousness, and they would ascend by spaceship. He began styling himself more and more as a Christ figure, a higher being put among mortals. Only through following him could his disciples achieve salvation. He also grew paranoid and stopped trying to find new converts, believing they might be servants of Lucifer attempting to infiltrate the group.

The group, now called Heaven's Gate, dwindled to 26 members at one point in the early 1990s. They increasingly saw the body, in particular sexual desires, as the enemy, and Applewhite and several of his followers underwent chemical castration. The higher beings of the next world would have no genitals, they believed.

In 1996, a photograph of the Hale-Bopp comet seemed to show a blurry object following behind. Applewhite believed the arrival of the comet was a sign he was right, and the blurry object was a spaceship to take his followers to the next plane of existence. He summoned them. Each took a barbiturate mixed with apple sauce, washed down with vodka. They then secured plastic bags around their heads. As each one died, those still alive would remove the plastic bag and lay the corpse on a bed. Applewhite was the third last to die – two followers were with him, and they were found still wearing the plastic bags. Three other members of the cult later killed themselves too. And the blurry object in the photograph was identified as a distant star, not a spaceship.

Was Applewhite evil, or did he believe he was doing an act of ultimate good? The paranoia and domineering manner of the last few years of his rule suggest that whatever pure motives he may have started with were no longer evident. In the end, 42 people killed themselves because of him, and one cult member who had escaped, Janja Lalich, was blunt. This was not suicide. It was murder.

CRIMINAL
MASTERMINDS

So many deaths. We have met some of the worst men in the world, and the number of bodies that have piled up is almost incomprehensible. The men in this final chapter may not have killed as many as those that have been discussed, and it can be easy to see them as less evil.

But each murder is horrific, and if suddenly the numbers seem small, it is only because we have allowed ourselves to be made immune to the reality of a single death. The criminal masterminds of our era tend to be drug traffickers, and the corpses they create can be hidden from view. But the traffickers know. And yet they continue to buy and sell, and they do so for one thing only: money.

In this they follow the lead of all criminal masterminds – they have, each and every one of them, decided that lining their own pockets is worth more than anything else. If more have to die for another briefcase of money, then more have to die.

To kill a human face to face is one thing, but these are men who have found more roundabout ways of doing it. The result remains the same: a corpse, its life cut short on the whim of another man, be it Osama bin Laden or Al Capone.

People speak of the lesser of two evils, and compared with many of those featured before, some of those in the rest of the book committed lesser evils. But a lesser evil is still an evil, and a corpse is still a corpse. And evil remains evil, however it is dealt.

OSAMA
BIN LADEN

It is an image that is burned into the minds of those who saw it, either in person or on television, and there is a strong argument that the world changed forever at that moment. On a bright Tuesday morning in New York in 2001, two commercial airliners brought down the Twin Towers of the World Trade Center, another hit the Pentagon, and a fourth was brought down by passengers as it headed toward Washington, possibly aiming at the Capitol Building, the seat of the US government.

Nineteen terrorists had hijacked the planes and used them to destroy some of the most important and iconic US buildings. It led to the War on Terror against militant Islamist movements and continues to shape our world. The events in which the 2,977 people died that day are well known, but what of the man who organized such an evil attack? Osama bin Laden was the mastermind of the deadliest, and most efficient, terror attack in history.

He was born in 1957 in Riyadh, Saudi Arabia. His father, Mohammed, was a billionaire construction worker, and his mother was Mohammed's tenth wife. Raised as a devout Muslim, bin Laden studied economics and business administration at university. He first married in 1974 at the age of 17 and had five other marriages, having somewhere between 20 and 26 children.

It was the Russian invasion of Afghanistan in 1979 that saw the devout Muslim become a radicalized one – he started to use his riches to fund resistance against the Soviets. When they were defeated and withdrew in 1988, he formed a new organization of Muslim resistance. Their name would go down in history – al-Qaeda, meaning "The Base". The group started to set up training camps and provided military and intelligence instruction in areas such as Afghanistan, Pakistan and Sudan.

At the training camps, recruits were trained for "jihad", meaning Holy War. They were taught military and guerilla tactics, how to fire guns, how to use bombs and, later, how to fly planes. In the event of a true Holy War, al-Qaeda would be ready. They might even start one.

Bin Laden left Saudi Arabia in 1991, citing that country's decision to use US troops against the threat of Iraq's Saddam Hussein. He viewed the US as more of a threat against Islam than Iraq and, from his new home in Sudan, started to direct his anger – and his firepower – against American forces and interests.

Expelled from Sudan in 1996 due to international pressure, he took refuge in Afghanistan. There he declared a fatwa, a Holy War, on the US. Bin Laden sought to draw the US into combat and, when they were defeated, impose a single Islamic state on the world.

In 1998, he made his first move – simultaneous bombings of US embassies in Kenya and Tanzania, in which 224 people were killed. Soon after, he bombed an American warship harboured in Yemen and killed 17 crew.

The success of these missions, as well as his charismatic videos calling for a rebirth of fundamentalist Islam against the infidel West, won him thousands of followers and new recruits. In 1999, he gathered together 19 of these recruits for a special mission. They were all well-educated, had lived in the West and spoke good English. They would be going to the US, he told them, where they would receive training to fly commercial airliners.

Later documents would show that bin Laden first conceived of the idea of what has become known as 9/11 after an Egyptian airliner had crashed into the sea, killing over 217 passengers in what was believed to be a deliberate act by the captain. If a plane crashing into the ocean could cause such damage, what about one crashing into a tower block in New York?

Bin Laden worked with the man later called the main architect of 9/11, Khalid Sheikh Mohammed. The targets were chosen, and the pilots commenced their training. While everything happened in great secrecy, a month before the attacks the CIA gave President George W. Bush a detailed report about a possible al-Qaeda attack organized by bin Laden, including "patterns of suspicious activity in this country consistent with preparations for a hijacking" of commercial aircraft. But nobody could have imagined what would happen that Tuesday morning.

Bin Laden initially denied responsibility – while he was immediately the chief suspect, it was not until 2004 that he would release a video in which he admitted he had orchestrated the attack. By then the hunt for him had been going for three years; it would last another seven. It was known that from

2005, he had been hiding in Pakistan. All attempts at capture or assassination had failed.

But on 2 May 2011, the then-president, Barack Obama, and his closest military advisers gathered in the Situation Room of the White House to watch live footage of a compound in Abbottabad, Pakistan. They observed as two dozen Navy SEALs in two Black Hawk helicopters landed at the compound and forced their way in. The raid lasted for 40 minutes. The SEALs found bin Laden as they rushed up to the third floor. Firing up the staircase, they hit him in the chest and head. Some SEALs claimed he tried to push one of his wives in front of him, but he was shot twice more in the forehead. They then contacted the Situation Room, with the code "EKIA" – Enemy Killed in Action. Or as President Obama put it, "We got him." Osama bin Laden was dead.

The body was placed in a body bag and taken to the USS Carl Vinson within 24 hours to be buried at sea. Also in the bag were 140 kgs of chains to ensure the bag sank. It was placed on a table, which was tipped forward, and the man who planned the 9/11 attacks was dropped to the bottom of the ocean.

PABLO ESCOBAR

They called him the King of Cocaine, and it is believed that he was worth around US$30 billion by the time of his death, making him perhaps the wealthiest criminal in history. He was undoubtedly the world's biggest drug trafficker during the 1980s and 1990s. The reign of Pablo Escobar was marked by extreme violence and corruption – not to forget the thousands of lives he took or ruined through drug use. And yet to some in Colombia he remains a hero – his funeral was attended by over 25,000 mourners, and his private estate, Hacienda Nápoles, from which he ran his empire, is now a theme park in his memory.

The son of a farmer and a schoolteacher, he was raised in extreme poverty in the Colombian city of Medellín. Even as a teenager he was engaged in a life of crime, including stealing tombstones, sandblasting their inscriptions and reselling them. He also turned to kidnapping – one ransom paid to him was $50,000 for the return of a businessman. But it soon became evident that the real money was elsewhere. Drugs.

In the 1970s, the cocaine industry in Colombia grew exponentially. Sourcing coca from Peru, Ecuador and Bolivia, gangs were making and selling cocaine in vast amounts. Escobar got in at the start of the growth and rode it better than anyone, without any ethical qualms about the drugs or the violence he used to get rid of opposition, either the authorities or other drug dealers. The Medellín Cartel, as it became known, was the most vicious gang of all.

As the money flowed in, up to an estimated $420 million a week, Escobar spent it freely on a lavish lifestyle. This included the 7,000-acre (2,800-hectare) Hacienda Nápoles estate. It cost $63 million and featured artificial lakes, a soccer field, dinosaur statues, an airstrip, a tennis court, even a bullfighting arena. There was also a zoo containing over 200 animals, including elephants, ostriches, zebras, camels and giraffes. His parties were famous, and his private planes grew ever more luxurious. He was not just the wealthiest criminal in the world – he was one of the wealthiest men.

Not that all of his money went on luxury. In the 1980s, he offered to pay off Colombia's entire $10 billion debt in return for exemption from any efforts by other countries to extradite him. He also engaged in philanthropy for the poor, paying for hospitals, soccer stadiums, parks, schools, churches and housing.

So rich was he that he often forgot how much cash he had or where he had put it. According to his brother, much of it was stored in warehouses and fields, with about $2.1 billion written off annually – because it had been lost, eaten by rats or destroyed by the elements. He was also rumoured to have burned $2 million one cold night in order to keep his daughter warm.

But what mustn't be forgotten is how he obtained all the money, whether or not he used it for good or evil. He handled problems with what he called *plata o plomo*, meaning "silver" (bribes) or "lead" (bullets). In 1989, the cartel used a bomb to blow a plane out of the sky because it contained an informer. The plane also contained 100 other people who died terrible deaths.

As Escobar's empire grew, so did the number of enemies, and his response was to kill first and ask questions later. Other cartel bosses were assassinated, and other drug traffickers paid with their lives for encroaching on his patch. He created an atmosphere of terror, with no one in any doubt as to what would happen if they got on his bad side.

By the 1990s, the US – which had lost citizens on the bombed plane and which was being flooded with drugs – sought Escobar's arrest and extradition. In June 1991, on the same day that the Colombian government voted to get rid of all extradition treaties, Escobar surrendered – no coincidence. He was then allowed by the government to build his own prison! Named La Catedral in Medellín, Colombia, it included a nightclub, sauna, waterfall, a giant dollhouse, a bar, a Jacuzzi and a soccer field! It was only when he tortured and killed two other drug dealers that he was sent to a regular prison – from which he immediately escaped.

By now Colombian authorities had had enough. A manhunt was launched, and on 1 December 1993 – Escobar's 44th birthday – his hideout was discovered using US technology. A major operation was launched, and the next day Escobar was shot on the roof attempting to flee, although some claimed he had killed himself. He was survived by his wife and two children.

There is one very strange legacy of Escobar. His zoo had been home to four hippopotamuses. They were too difficult to capture from the zoo when he died, so they were left to roam. Four became 16, which then became 40. These animals have left a path of destruction, attacking cattle and destroying crops. Attempts to castrate the males to stop breeding have met with limited success. Even all these years after his death, Pablo Escobar's trail of destruction continues to grow – though not as evil as the drug dealing, of course...

LUCKY LUCIANO

The Mafia. It's a word that still inspires fear. There are as many variations as there are countries, but two strands stand out. One is the original Sicilian Mafia, known as the Cosa Nostra ("Our Thing"), which emerged in the nineteenth century, initially as a private army to oversee disputes and later as a criminal gang.

The other strand was created in the US by an impoverished population of Italian immigrants, particularly around New York. And no one was more influential in bringing what would also be called "The Mob" to the US than Salvatore Lucania, also known as Charles Luciano, but mostly known as Lucky. The blueprint Lucky Luciano set out for the US Mafia – the sharp suits, the guns, the language, the attitude – all came from Lucky. It is not for nothing that the word "mafia" means "swagger".

Born in Sicily in 1897, Luciano emigrated with his family to the US in 1906 when he was eight years old, settling in Manhattan. At the age of ten, he was already in trouble for mugging and shoplifting. At 14, he dropped out of school and joined various gangs, offering protection to Jewish boys and other Italians for ten cents a week, and at 16, he was jailed for the first time for selling heroin.

With the 1920 Prohibition Act leading to a ban on the manufacture, sale and transportation of alcoholic beverages, a black market sprang up, and criminal gangs became bootleggers. Luciano became a gunman for the emerging crime boss, Joe Masseria, and ran the bootlegging business. With that, and the drug running and prostitution rings he was controlling, Luciano's wealth grew rapidly. And by 1925, aged just 28, he was earning over $12 million per year, astonishing money for that time.

By now he was Masseria's second-in-command and took part in the bloody Mafia wars of the late 1920s and early 1930s. It nearly cost him his life – in October 1929, he was abducted by a rival gang, stabbed repeatedly with an ice pick and had his throat slit. He survived, and the legend of "Lucky" was born.

He had soon had enough of the Mafia war – which was bad for business – and of being Masseria's lieutenant. He lured Masseria to a restaurant and had him mown down by four loyalists. Others who stood in Luciano's way were executed on his orders, including the other big crime boss of the time, Salvatore Maranzano, who was stabbed multiple times and then shot. Others were killed in particularly sadistic ways. Luciano didn't just want them dead; he wanted them to be an example and to make others fear him.

By 1934, there was no doubt – Lucky Luciano was the head of the Mafia, or the *capo di tutti capi* – the "boss of all bosses". He immediately abolished this title, believing it would lead to ambitious challengers. Instead, he formed what he called "The Commission", the governing body of the American Mafia, consisting of the bosses of the Five Mafia Families of New York City.

Law enforcement was by now tailing Luciano, in particular the special prosecutor Thomas Dewey, who was responsible for a whole slew of arrests in the 1920s and 1930s. In 1936, Dewey led raids on brothels throughout the city, arresting more than 100 people, mostly women. Many gave evidence against Luciano in return for their freedom. On 6 June 1936, Luciano was convicted of 62 charges of prostitution; he was sentenced to 30–50 years in state prison.

From prison he continued to run his evil empire, having enemies slain and spreading drugs and prostitution throughout America. But it turned out the US also needed Lucky Luciano. After entering the Second World War in 1941, the country had to avoid strikes among dockworkers, as well as requiring heightened security around their boats to avoid attacks. With his contacts Luciano helped coordinate both of these things, in return for being released at the end of the war. He was duly let out in 1946 on the condition that he would leave the US. He moved first to Cuba and then back to his native Italy, where he continued to direct the drug traffic into the US and the smuggling of fellow Italians to America. Those who crossed him continued to be sent to "sleep with the fishes".

As for Lucky Luciano, he didn't die in any hail of gunfire but of a heart attack in 1962 at an airport on his way to talk to a director about a film based on his life. Three days later 300 people attended a funeral service for Luciano in Naples. His body was shipped back to New York, the king returning to his kingdom.

BERNIE MADOFF

He was known as the Monster of Wall Street, but in a documentary of that name, one of his victims is blunter, calling him "a financial sociopath, a serial financial killer". In the blizzard of numbers around Bernie Madoff, it is easy to forget the trail of death and destruction he left, as many of those whose lives he ruined chose suicide as their only option.

We don't know how many suicides were caused by Madoff or how many he sent to financial ruin. Every investor story is one of losing houses, losing relationships, losing the chance to retire and, in the worst cases, losing their loves. Madoff knew this as he piled up the money. Every dollar he had was one he took, and as he loved the high life, others suffered.

His scheme was staggering in its simplicity but no less evil for that. He convinced investors to send money with which he claimed he would play the market. This is completely legitimate – the stock market is built on it. Instead, he simply placed the money in a bank account. When some people wanted their money plus earnings back, he would pay out, knowing most investors would keep their money with him. It gave his business an appearance of legitimacy.

By definition, Madoff had to get more and more investors to cover any payouts comfortably and to keep growing his account. The true number of investors he defrauded will never be known, but at the time of his arrest in 2008, he had around $823 million in a bank account in his wife Ruth's name. But that is a tiny fraction of how much he actually took – on conviction he was ordered to forfeit $170 billion in assets.

Madoff's enterprise had a history – it is known as a Ponzi scheme, named for the Italian immigrant Charles Ponzi, who did a similar thing in the 1920s, taking around $20 million from investors. Jailed and deported, Ponzi spent the last few years of his life in poverty.

Madoff's own Ponzi scheme collapsed in late 2008 when the financial crisis of that year saw the stock market collapse. A large number of Madoff's investors, thinking they had stocks which were dropping in price, wanted to withdraw their money. Madoff didn't have anywhere near enough to cover them. Attempts to dissuade investors failed. On 10 December 2008, Madoff confessed his sins to his sons. A day later they turned him over to authorities.

He was born in New York in 1938, his parents emigrants from Eastern Europe. His father was a plumber and then a stockbroker. Madoff received a Bachelor of Arts in political science, briefly attended law school and then set up Bernard L. Madoff Investment Securities in 1960 at the age of 22, often working with his brother, Peter.

The firm was successful, and by the late 1980s, Madoff was making in the vicinity of $100 million a year. In 2001, the firm made headlines for its involvement in creating Nasdaq, the first digital version of the stock market, which became the most active stock trading venue in the US by volume. Madoff was its chairman three times. Also in 2001, the Madoff firm was incorporated as a limited liability company, with Madoff as the sole shareholder.

It was in 1999 that concerns were first raised against Madoff, then seen as a respectable businessman and great innovator. Financial analyst Harry Markopolos informed the Securities and Exchange Commission (SEC) that it was impossible for Madoff to be making the profits he claimed. The SEC ignored him. In addition, none of the major Wall Street firms invested with him, believing his returns were at best inflated, at worst false. Others grew suspicious that a three-person company, with only one accountant, could manage the sort of investment portfolio Madoff had. But still, until his sons turned him over in 2008, nothing was done.

On 19 November 2008, Madoff had just enough money in his wife's account to pay investors who wanted to withdraw from the market. But the requests kept coming. The account, which had over $5.5 billion in mid-2008, was down to $234 million in November, not enough to cover even a fraction of the outstanding redemptions. In addition, banks had frozen all major lending. Madoff could not even borrow money to give to investors. He finally confessed.

He asked his sons to give him a week to wind up operations before going to the police – but as soon as they left him, they went to the authorities. Bernie Madoff was arrested on 11 December. He was charged with fraud and sentenced to 150 years in jail. Aged 71, he knew he would die in jail, which he did in April 2014 at the age of 82. His accountant received one year of home detention in return for giving evidence. Madoff's right-hand man, Frank DiPascali, was due to receive 125 years, but he died before sentencing.

The job of trying to reclaim the money also began, but it was hugely complicated, and the majority of investors were left with their livelihoods and lives destroyed – of the almost 20,000 claimants, three-quarters would see none of their money returned.

His body was cremated, and his ashes remain in a box in his lawyer's office – his family refused to receive them.

ALEXANDER SOLONIK

His nickname says it all – Superkiller. When Alexander Solonik was given your name to wipe out, that was the end of you. There is no one in the Russian Mafia who you would particularly like to meet on a dark night, so the fact that he was known as the most feared among the Mafia gives some idea of the sort of man he was. That and the fact that when he was attacked by 12 inmates in prison who found out he had briefly worked as a police officer, he won the fight.

He was specific in his targets – other Mob bosses – and ruthless in his execution. Nothing was allowed to get in his way. Take the case of Valeri Dlugatsj. In 1992, Dlugatsj was at a nightclub he owned, surrounded by a phalanx of bodyguards. Lesser killers than Solonik would have been put off. Superkiller had no such qualms – he simply walked in, shot Dlugatsj and made his escape, dodging the bullets of the bodyguards as they flew at him.

He was born in 1960 in the Soviet Russian city of Kurgan, and even as a child he was interested in martial arts and guns.

On finishing school, he was conscripted to serve in tanks for the Soviet Forces in Germany. On leaving the service, he joined the police force, but after six months he was expelled for discrediting the force by using extreme violence when questioning suspects. There are rumours some of them died – his first victims.

In 1987, after two marriages which produced a child each, he was charged with the rape of another woman and sentenced to eight years in prison. He escaped by jumping from the second floor of the jail. Captured soon after, he was placed in solitary confinement for his own protection, given his past as a police officer. But after a time, he was moved to the general prison – which is when he faced the posse of 12 inmates and overpowered them. We don't know how, but we do know no one attacked him ever again.

Two years later he escaped again and started working as a hitman, initially around his hometown of Kurgan, where he joined a criminal organization aligned with the Mafia. His skill was immediately recognized – he had no fear and could shoot equally well with both hands. He was a perfect killing machine.

His first murder outside the police force was in 1990, the boss of a rival organization, and his second was in 1992, Viktor Nikiforov, also in the Mob. Valeri Dlugatsj was next, his night out at the nightclub ended abruptly by Solonik. When Dlugatsj was replaced by Vladislav Vinner, Solonik killed Vinner too.

Solonik was by now being called Superkiller, and no one with their fingers in the pie of Russian criminal money felt safe. Acting on a tip-off, police tracked him down to a marketplace where he was having a drink. Foolishly, they failed to search him thoroughly before they brought him into the station – there he pulled out a Glock 17 pistol, shooting three officers and then running outside, where he gunned down another two. He himself was shot in the kidney and then captured. This time the police were more vigilant about checking him for weapons and took away his gun.

Solonik confessed to a large number of crimes, many of which he could not have committed. It is rumoured that he confessed to them in order to have the police carry out investigations, then he could use the information they found to track other kills.

He was sentenced to life in prison, but the authorities couldn't hold onto him for long – in 1995, he again escaped, using climbing equipment that had been smuggled in to rappel down the prison wall. Remarkably, a mannequin had also been smuggled into the jail, and he left it in his bed, so his disappearance was not noticed for hours.

He was now on Russia's Top Ten Wanted list, and a massive search took place across Russia. It was to no avail – Solonik had managed to get to Greece, where he set up his own criminal syndicate with about 50 members. Buying several villas in Athens to store a massive arsenal of guns, the syndicate specialized in drug running and contract killings. It is not known how "hands-on" Solonik was with the latter, but it is unlikely the Superkiller could resist showing off his skills.

It was in January 1997 that he finally got what was coming to him when he was taken out by another hitman in one of his villas. His body was found strangled to death. Superkiller was as dead as his victims.

Or was he? Rumours persist that he faked his own death, as no fingerprint identification took place. Could it be that Alexander Solonik evaded the law yet again?

LIU ZHAOHUA

He was known as the Ice King, after the drug that made his name, the crystal methamphetamine known as "ice". Stronger than "speed" and much deadlier, it became the party drug of choice in parts of the world in the 1990s. And whoever took any had a fair chance that they were putting money into the coffers of the Chinese drug lord Liu Zhaohua.

How much ice did Liu make? An astonishing 31 tonnes. And how much is that? An average car weighs .4 of a tonne, which means that he produced the weight of nearly 80 cars of small white powder. And how much is that worth? Estimates put the cost at US$5.5 billion. And how much is that? If you could save $100,000 a year, it would take you 55,000 years to save $5.5 billion. That's a lot of money, and a lot of drugs.

Born in 1965, Liu showed an early interest in chemistry, which would hold him in good stead later. At 14, he won a chemistry prize. But soon after, he was forced to drop out of school due to his family's poverty. He joined the army and served for four years. He then moved into business and encountered the new wonder drug, crystal meth, for the first time. He decided to make it himself.

While keeping his day job, Liu started producing the drug in his own home. Early results were unpromising, and he sought advice on how to make better stuff. He disguised himself as a researcher looking into weight loss products and was shown by a university professor how to make better and stronger methamphetamines. Flushed with his success, he founded Fujian Hongfa Plastic, a plastic processing company which acted as the front for his drug business. He used his daytime business contacts to help distribute the drugs.

By 1986, he had earned enough to build a factory, but when this was raided, he went on the run – the penalty for anyone in China who has produced more than 50 grams of illegal drugs is either 15 years in prison, life imprisonment or death. The police found 11 tonnes, 22 million times that amount.

Liu moved to Puning, Guangdong, where he continued operations while hiding under an alias. By 1999, he had opened two additional factories. He was also using his alias to attempt to move back into society, appearing on television posing as a successful businessman and starting a biotech corporation for the cultivation of yew trees.

But drugs remained his main trade. We can't know how many deaths were caused by ice, but one US report estimated 1,800 deaths caused by methamphetamine abuse from 1992 to 1994 in California alone. Added to this are the number of lives ruined by drugs, those who suffered physical and mental damage, and the casualties suffered in crimes associated with trafficking. Liu knew all of this but continued operations.

There was by now a large reward for information which would help arrest Liu, and on 5 March 2005, his 40th birthday, Liu was tracked down to a rented apartment after a tip-off. He was arrested for the possession and manufacture of the

18 tonnes of methamphetamines that could be found – even this amount far outweighed all the other methamphetamines seized in the world that year. One police officer who had seen the factory said, "At the processing plant, there were automatic control panels and dozens of reaction tanks. It was just phenomenal. We had never seen anything like that before."

Displaying an arrogance that he was known for by associates, even after he was arrested Liu taunted police officers and assured them that he would be set free. He claimed he had, in fact, been making rat poison, not drugs, and that he should be released.

No one believed him. He was sentenced to death, and on 15 September 2009, he was executed, joining in death many of those who had sampled his product.

AL CAPONE

His nickname, Scarface. His beat, Chicago. It is scarcely believable that this legend of US folklore only spent seven years as a crime boss and was only 33 when he was famously arrested for tax evasion, which was easier to prove than the rest of his crimes.

We will never know how many men went to their graves at the command of Al Capone, but we know seven of them met their end during the infamous St Valentine's Day Massacre of 14 February 1929, lined up against a warehouse wall and machine-gunned to death. They were all members of the North Side Gang, Capone's chief rivals for control of Chicago. Before the massacre, Capone was feted as a hero, being cheered in the streets and at baseball games. After it, he was Public Enemy Number 1 – the first in history to be given the designation that would later be applied to such evil men as Osama bin Laden and Joaquín "El Chapo" Guzmán, both featured in this book.

Born as one of nine children in Brooklyn in 1899 to Italian immigrants – Capone's father was a barber and his mother a seamstress – Capone worked odd jobs after his expulsion from school before meeting Italian-born mobster Johnny

Torrio, moving to Chicago and joining his gang. In 1920, when prohibition came in, the gang worked as bootleggers, but they also ran prostitution rings and were involved in "transportation". In newspaper articles of the time, Capone is listed as a boxing promoter.

They also became involved in gang wars, and in January 1925, Capone was ambushed but survived, and then 12 days later, Torrio was shot several times. Seriously wounded, Torrio retired to Brooklyn. Capone was now boss, and he set out to eliminate his rivals and take revenge for the attacks on him and Torrio, building a fearsome reputation for his cold-blooded methods and the ruthlessness of his operations.

He also became a local and then national celebrity, setting the template for crime bosses in any number of books and films. He dressed in expensive suits, wore expensive jewellery, had expensive girlfriends. He claimed he was just a humble businessman giving the people what they wanted. Booze and glamour.

All of that changed on Valentine's Day, 1929. Capone had an ongoing dispute with Bugs Moran, head of the North Side Gang, which came to a head when that gang stole some expensive whisky that Capone's gang had smuggled in illegally from Canada. Moran had also attempted to muscle in on some of Capone's dog tracks and saloons. Also, his gang was not Italian and therefore automatically suspect.

Capone lured the North Side Gang members to a warehouse on North Clark Street with the promise of a load of cheap whisky, which was supplied by Detroit's Purple Gang, associates of Capone. Bugs Moran was supposed to be among their number but was running late. They arrived at approximately 10.30 a.m.

Soon after, a van drove in, blocking the exit. Two men dressed as policemen got out, telling the North Side Gang members they were under arrest and had to go and stand against a wall. Two other men in plain clothes got out of the van. They were carrying Thompson submachine guns. They sprayed the gang members with bullets, not stopping when the bodies hit the ground. They then left on foot, with the two men in plain clothes putting their hands up and walking ahead of the men dressed as police.

The real police arrived shortly after – Bugs Moran, approaching the warehouse, saw them and fled. The only survivors were a gang member's dog, Highball, and a gang member, Frank Gusenberg, despite 14 bullet wounds. Taken to hospital, he refused to name names and died three hours later.

But no one was in any doubt who ordered the killings. Capone had overplayed his hand – the national celebrity was now the nation's most hated man. It also caused problems for the other organizations in the National Crime Syndicate, a confederation of crime groups. Both the law and the criminal underworld were now his enemies.

Forced to testify for a week to a Grand Jury investigating criminal activity in March 1929, Capone was arrested as he left for contempt of court and released on $5,000 bail. Then, on 17 May, he and his bodyguard were arrested for having concealed weapons. Each received a year in prison – Capone served nine months and was released for good behaviour on 17 March 1930. He then served six months for contempt of court.

All the while, police were gathering evidence to try and tie Capone to the massacre. They were up against the criminals' code, which meant no one would testify against him, no matter how much they wanted him brought to justice. But for all the investigations and arrests, no one was ever formally charged – including Al Capone.

In the end, they gave up. But US Assistant Attorney General Mabel Walker Willebrandt had a brilliant idea. You didn't need an informer to catch a criminal on a tax evasion rap. By tracking Capone's spending, they could show it was more than he claimed his income was. The rest of his income must be illegal. In 1931, the government charged Capone with evasion of $215,000 in taxes on a total income of $1,038,654. He was found guilty and, in May 1932, was sentenced to 11 years in prison.

The feared crime boss became a weak and scared man in prison. Never physically imposing, without his bodyguards and guns he became the subject of bullying and physical assaults. He also suffered terribly from cocaine withdrawal and the gradual onset of the symptoms of syphilis, which caused mental health issues. His health was so bad that he was released in 1939. He spent the rest of his life in and out of hospital and would become one of the first people in the US to receive penicillin. It slowed down his mental deterioration but did not stop it. According to physicians, by 1946, he had the mentality of a 12-year-old. And in 1947, his heart failed. He was buried in Chicago, the city he once held in the palm of his hand, but which now took him into its ground a broken man, unmourned.

JOAQUÍN "EL CHAPO" GUZMÁN

One for the next dinner party – what is the most cash ever seized at the same time by law enforcement in history? The answer is staggering. When Mexican authorities raided a property linked to the Sinaloa Drug Cartel, they found US$205 million. The money was hidden in suitcases, closets and behind walls. Everywhere they looked in the house they found more cash. The most powerful drug trafficking organization in the Western Hemisphere, with tentacles in over 50 countries, did not know what to do with all its money.

But it is not the only staggering figure to do with the cartel. There is also the question of the number of deaths that its leader, Joaquín "El Chapo" Guzmán, was responsible for. According to Forbes magazine, when you include drug deaths and the many casualties from Mexico's drug wars, up to 34,000 people were killed due to El Chapo. No wonder the US government called him "the most ruthless, dangerous, and feared man on the planet" and made him Public Enemy Number 1.

He was a small man – El Chapo means "Shorty" – who had ascended to the top of the Mexican drug trade despite being born in 1957 to a poor family of farmers, including a father who regularly beat him. Guzmán started cultivating and selling marijuana as a young man. He worked for the Guadalajara Cartel, which became infamous when they kidnapped and tortured to death a US intelligence officer, Enrique Camarena Salazar, who had organized a raid on their plantation.

By the late 1980s, Guzmán had his own cartel, the Sinaloa Cartel, dealing in harder drugs, including marijuana, heroin, cocaine and methamphetamine. US authorities believed that from 19 October 1987 to 18 May 1990, he had coordinated the shipment of 2,000 kg (4,400 lb) of marijuana and about 4,700 kg (10,400 lb) of cocaine by land, air and through tunnels from Mexico to America.

A dispute with another cartel, the Tijuana Cartel, showed El Chapo at his most ruthless. On 3 September 1992, nine members of the opposing cartel were killed, including their lawyers. After a hit on Guzmán himself failed, he tracked three leaders of the enemy cartel to a discothèque in Puerto Vallarta. His gunmen opened fire at them. The shooting lasted for at least eight minutes, and more than 1,000 rounds were fired. Six people died. Then, on 9 and 10 December 1992, four alleged associates of the cartel's leader were killed.

Arrested for the first time in 1993 in Guatemala, where he was hiding, El Chapo was extradited to Mexico and sentenced to 20 years and nine months in prison on charges of drug trafficking, criminal association and bribery – it wasn't possible to make the murder charges stick. He continued to run his empire from prison, and such was his power that he was granted a luxurious lifestyle, with prison guards acting as servants. He also met a new mistress, former police officer Zulema Hernández, who was serving time for armed robbery. The pair were given the run of the prison.

In 2001, he escaped with the help of corrupt prison guards. The escape allegedly cost Guzmán $2.5 million in bribes. By now the Sinaloa Cartel was the wealthiest and most powerful of Mexico's drug cartels, ferrying tonnes of cocaine across the border to its drug gangs in America. El Chapo was ranked the tenth richest man in Mexico and 1,140th in the world in 2011, with a net worth of roughly US$1 billion.

Such was the gang's influence that they bribed Juan Orlando Hernández with the millions of dollars that helped him become President of Honduras in 2013. By then the manhunt for the first man to be declared Public Enemy Number 1 in the US since Lucky Luciano had been going for a decade. Various major arrests of drug dealers and traffickers in Mexico left El Chapo untouched – they even helped him eliminate rivals. So much so that many thought the authorities were helping Guzmán in return for money and political favours.

He escaped from law enforcement using armoured cars and aircraft – it is rumoured his bodyguards had surface-to-air missiles – and used sophisticated technology to warn him of attacks. His reputation as a man impossible to catch grew and grew. All the while he engaged in battles against other cartels, which often ended up with the murder of the cartel's head and, on more than one occasion, their whole family.

His luck nearly ran out on 16 February 2014, when the Mexican military traced him to the house of an ex-wife – but even that had a steel-reinforced front door, and El Chapo made his escape through a network of tunnels as the soldiers continued to try and force entry.

The operation that finally caught him, a week later at a hotel resort, was the biggest in Mexican history – in fact, it is hard to imagine a bigger operation to bring down one man anywhere, any time. Ten pickup trucks of the Mexican Navy carrying over 65 marines made their way to the resort, aware that El Chapo was on the fourth floor, in Room 401. He was found in bed with his new wife, American beauty contest winner Emma Coronel Aispuro. He was arrested at 6.40 a.m., without any shots being fired, and charged with drug trafficking only, as more evidence was gathered of other crimes.

But then, on 11 July 2015, he did it again – El Chapo escaped, this time through a tunnel under his shower. The tunnel was equipped with artificial light, air ducts and high-quality construction materials. And, deeper down, a motorcycle. The Sinaloa Cartel had done it again.

On 8 January 2016, 17 marines from the Mexican Navy's Special Forces identified El Chapo in a house in the coastal city of Los Mochis in northern Sinaloa. As they stormed the building, he again escaped through a tunnel, emerging to steal a car at gunpoint. Most of the Mexican army and police force tracked the vehicle, and he was finally arrested just 20 kilometres away. He told the authorities that 40 of his men were on the way to free him, but the police hid him in a motel.

A criminal in Mexico, he remained the US' most wanted man, and the US managed to extradite him on 19 January 2017. He was charged with drug trafficking, money laundering, corruption and murder. The trial took two years to complete, and on 12 February 2019, he was found guilty of all charges and was sentenced to life plus 30 years in prison.

The man who killed 34,000 people had finally been put where he could do no more damage, take no more lives –

ADX Florence, the most secure supermax prison in the US, in solitary confinement for 23 hours a day. No tunnels, no guns, no motorcycles. And no drugs.

GIUSEPPE GRECO

He who lives by the gun…

Many men have been sentenced to life in prison for their crimes. But not many have been given the sentence after they are dead. But when the high-ranking member of the Sicilian Mafia, Giuseppe Greco, was sentenced to die in prison in 1987, he was already two years dead – killed by his fellow Mafiosi for being too crazy, even by their standards.

In one way, Greco – known as Pino, short for Giuseppe – didn't stand a chance. He was, in fact, the son of a Mafia hitman named "Scarpa", meaning "shoe", and Greco was originally known as "Scarpuzzedda", meaning "little shoe". But his exploits would eventually leave his father's reputation for, dare we say it, dead. Starting out as a driver for Kalsa clan boss Tommaso Spadaro, Greco ended up joining the Sicilians and became one of the top hitmen – and most prolific killers – in Mafia history.

Born in Sicily in 1952, he was an intelligent student, excelling in Latin and Greek. But a life of books was not for him. He started in small crime and then graduated to working for the big crime bosses of the time. But it was in the famous Second Mafia War from 1981 to 1984 that he was to make his reputation. The war, also known as the "Mattanza", meaning "slaughter", left thousands dead – mafiosi, judges, detectives, activists and politicians. And none had more blood on his hands than Pino Greco.

How many did Greco kill? At his trial he was charged with 58 murders, but the number in which he was the chief suspect was closer to 80. And the number many in the criminal underworld ascribed to him is closer to 300.

One example – in 1985, Greco gunned down three police officers, Stefano Bontade, Salvatore Inzerillo and Pio La Torre. The 15-year-old son of Inzerillo was foolish enough to say to the press that he would avenge the death of his father, Hollywood-style. But the streets of Sicily are not Hollywood. Greco tracked the boy down, tortured him, and then cut his arm off. He then shot the boy in the head and dissolved his corpse in acid.

Meanwhile, Greco was on the trail of Salvatore Contorno, a former member of the Sicilians, who had turned state witness. Greco shot him in the chest, but Contorno was wearing a bulletproof vest supplied by authorities. Contorno then disappeared into hiding. Greco was undeterred – he gradually killed all of Contorno's friends and family. If he couldn't kill the man himself, he would dispose of everything he cared about.

Greco's immediate boss was Salvatore Riina. Under his patronage, Greco gradually built a "death squad" of some of the most brutal killers in the Mafia. They instigated a number of massacres that would go down in history and folklore – the 25 December 1981 "Christmas Massacre" (four deaths); the 16 June 1982 "Circonvallazione massacre" (five deaths); and the 3 September 1982 "Via Carini massacre" (three deaths). All were done in the open – Greco had no fear.

He also worked with the notorious Filippo Marchese, who ran what was known as the "Room of Death", where victims were tortured and murdered before being thrown into vats of acid or dismembered and then dumped in the sea. Greco enjoyed garrotting his victims while another mafiosi held their feet.

Greco and Marchese were responsible for the death of Rosario Riccobono, the Cosa Nostra's king of drug trafficking. In November 1982, they invited Riccobono and eight of his men to a barbeque. On the orders of their boss, Salvatore Riina, they gunned down the men and then strangled Riccobono – he was surplus to requirements as far as Riina was concerned. Soon after, Marchese was also declared unmercenary, and Greco had no qualms about murdering his close friend and ally.

Greco was by now head of one of the Sicilian families, the Ciaculli family. But he was also becoming increasingly unhinged, setting off bombs and shooting men on a whim. He killed for no apparent reason and usually tortured his victims first. He was getting out of any control, least of all Riina's. Riina responded by having a large swathe of the Ciaculli family gunned down to remind Little Shoe that his power was limited.

But Greco continued his indiscriminate killing. And so, sometime in September 1985, the 33-year-old Pino Greco was shot to death in his own home. Riina ordered the body to be dissolved in acid. He told other members of the Sicilian families that Greco had fled to the US.

The Mafia War ended with what is known as the Maxi Trial. Lasting six years, it saw 475 mafiosi charged, with 338 jailed for a total of 2,665 years – the largest trial in history. One of those tried in absentia was Pino Greco, and he received a life sentence. Only later was it revealed that he was already long dead. When Riina was asked why he had killed one of his best assassins, he said that he had found the medicine for madmen – Little Shoe was no normal hitman – he had, said Riina, gone crazy.

THE KRAY TWINS

We generally think of criminal masterminds as having huge intelligence, rat-like cunning and running a hugely sophisticated organization. But surely, if you reshape an entire community in your image, inspire fear and turn into cultural legends while doing so, isn't that also a type of huge intelligence? By that definition, the Kray twins, Reggie and Ronnie, were as clever at what they did as any evil genius.

More than 50 years since the height of their terror, the pair's names are still spoken in hushed tones in London's rough and tumble East End, where they ruled with an iron fist from the late 1950s to their arrest in 1968. As the rest of London was going through the Swinging Sixties, this pocket of the capital was having a much darker time of it as the Kray twins' criminal gang, known as The Firm, involved itself in armed robbery, protection rackets, arson, gambling, assault and, of course, murder.

They were born identical twins on 24 October 1933 in East London, and their parents were East London born and bred. Reggie was minutes older than Ronnie, and they had an older brother of six, Charles, who was a boxer and also had a life of crime, although he was most famous for dating Barbara Windsor, star of the Carry On films.

The family was ruled over by the Krays' mother, Violet – their father, a rag-and-bone man, was usually absent, and when war broke out in 1939, he went AWOL, remaining a fugitive until his arrest in 1954. Violet spoiled the boys and told them they were special – she proved to be right.

After a brief spell in the army – like their father, they went AWOL and spent time in prison for it, with a psychiatrist declaring Ronnie "educationally subnormal, psychopathic, schizophrenic and insane" – the Kray twins set up as nightclub owners in the 1950s. The club was a front for various criminal activities. They ran a protection racket extorting money from businesses in exchange for keeping their property safe from burning down and carried out a series of armed robberies. They also began money laundering through greyhound and horse racing.

But it was their personal violence that earned them their fearsome reputation. Ronnie was especially barbaric and, unlike Reggie, seemed to lose control at the slightest provocation. Once, in 1954, he attacked a whole rival gang with a cutlass, and in 1956, he spent three years in prison for stabbing a man with a bayonet. His behaviour was so erratic and dangerous in prison that he was administered sedatives constantly and diagnosed with paranoid schizophrenia.

On the outside, Reggie was building their empire, combining criminal activities with other projects that gave The Firm a veneer of respectability. He bought a new club among the theatres in London's West End, and when Ronnie was released, the pair became London celebrities, as actors and musicians frequented their establishment. Frank Sinatra, Sammy Davis Jr and Cliff Richard all made an appearance. With their legitimate and illegitimate businesses both thriving, the Krays saw themselves as untouchable.

Even as the empire grew – the twins dreamed of setting up their own version of the American Mafia – Ronnie's unpredictable and violent behaviour grew more troubling. When he heard a rival gang member, George Cornell, was drinking at a pub on Kray turf, he went straight there and, in front of everyone, shot Cornell in the head. But such was the Krays' reputation that everyone in the pub said they could not identify the killer.

It was when Reggie, long thought to be the steady hand in the relationship, committed a flagrant murder that things collapsed. He had begun drinking heavily to deal with the stress of the business. His wife of two years, Frances Shea, was also attempting to have the marriage annulled, claiming he was violent and that the marriage had never been consummated. Under the pressure of trying to escape the marriage, she committed suicide in 1967, aged 23.

Four months later the Kray twins lured a member of The Firm, Jack "the Hat" McVitie, to a basement flat in Stoke Newington. McVitie had failed to carry out a hit for which he had been paid half, £500, in advance. Reggie tried to shoot McVitie, but his gun jammed. In a fury, no doubt helped along by his failed marriage and the suicide of his wife, the normally cool Reggie grabbed a knife and stabbed McVitie over and over again, finally impaling him to the floor with a carving knife through the throat. McVitie's body was never found.

The brutality of the murder, and the fact that it was against a member of The Firm, shocked their other "employees". People began to snitch on the pair, going to the police with more stories of violence and murder. Suddenly several of the people in the pub when Cornell was shot could, in fact, identify the killer.

Early in 1968, the police arrested an associate of The Firm, Paul Elvey, who was on his way to Glasgow to buy explosives for a car bomb. He confessed to being involved in three attempted murders, all organized by the Krays. The police swept in, rightly believing that once the Krays were behind bars, others would come forward and give evidence against them. On 8 May 1968, the Krays and 15 members of The Firm were arrested.

Reggie and Ronnie Kray were charged with the murders of Cornell and McVitie, among other charges. Their trial was the longest murder trial in British history, and it was so sensational that seats in the court were being sold for £5, worth hundreds of pounds in current money. The twins were both found guilty and sentenced to 30 years in prison each, the judge declaring, "In my view, society has earned a rest from your activities."

Reggie Kray remained in prison until 2000. He was released on compassionate grounds due to illness a few weeks before his death on 1 October, aged 66, of terminal bladder cancer. Ronnie, who was marked as a Category A prisoner, not allowed to mix with others, was certified insane in 1979 and spent the remainder of his life in a high-security psychiatric hospital, dying of a heart attack in March 1995, aged 61.

But even behind bars they stayed in business – in 1985, they were found to be running "Krayleigh Enterprises", supplying bodyguards to celebrities. One client employed 18 of their bodyguards that year in order to attend Wimbledon – their old drinking buddy, Frank Sinatra.

ADAM WORTH

They called him "The Napoleon of Crime", and like the French general and emperor, no country could contain him or his legend. Europe, Africa, the US – there were few places on Earth that did not, at one time or another, find themselves duped or swindled by Adam Worth. So notorious did he become that he inspired the arch nemesis of Arthur Conan Doyle's Sherlock Holmes – the greatest criminal mastermind in fiction, Moriarty.

But no fiction could do justice to the wizardry of Worth.

He was born in Germany in about 1844, although no one quite knows where. His family were poor, but they managed to emigrate to the US when he was five, his father becoming a tailor. At the age of 14, he ran away from home, first to Boston and then to New York. He did not go back. In 1861, at the age of 17, he joined the Union Army and fought in the Civil War. When he was mistakenly declared dead in August 1862, he saw the opportunity to go AWOL. He also saw the opportunity to make money.

He became a bounty jumper. At the time, there was conscription in the Union, but wealthy families could pay men $1,000 to serve in their place. By using aliases, Worth received several bounties, leaving the army again each time as soon as he could. When the authorities finally got wise, he fled back to New York, where he became involved in the criminal underworld, organizing a gang of pickpockets. He also stole a cash box from a train and was sentenced to three years in prison. He escaped immediately; no one could work out how.

Newly free – and with a new moustache and mutton chops as a disguise – he started to work for legendary criminal fence (someone who buys and sells stolen goods) Fredericka "Marm" Mandelbaum. Worth quickly grew frustrated at how amateurish many attempts at robberies were and started working at refining techniques for getting away with loot. His methods proved effective, and the term "criminal mastermind" was born.

One example of his combination of meticulous planning and daring – in 1869, he decided to rob the Boylston National Bank in Boston with his new partner, Charles Bullard, who Worth had helped escape from jail. What they didn't do was run into the bank wielding guns. What they did do was set up a fake health tonic shop next door, then spend months digging a tunnel through the wall and under the vault, and then popping in and taking all the money. It was brilliant, breathtaking stuff.

It was also the sort of thing that gets you talked about, and the pair were soon on the police's watchlist. It was then that Worth and Bullard decided in 1870 that there was too much heat and left the US for Europe.

They spent time in Liverpool, where they met and formed a tryst with a barmaid named Kitty Flynn, who gave birth to two daughters, with both men possible fathers, although she married Bullard. After a year of petty crime, the trio moved to Paris together. There they opened an illegal gambling den, with ingenious apparatus that hid the equipment if the gendarmes arrived. Even so, they were regularly raided and decided to close up and head to London.

Astonishingly, Worth then managed two things – he set up a criminal organization, and he joined high society! As "Henry J. Raymond" he associated with some of the greatest nobility in England while at the same time organizing major robberies, often from the very people he was taking tea with of an afternoon.

His most audacious theft was that of the famous painter Thomas Gainsborough's recently rediscovered painting of the Duchess of Devonshire. It had been purchased for 10,000 guineas by art dealer William Agnew in 1876, the highest price ever paid for a painting in history, close to £2 million in today's money. But having promised to sell it to help pay the men who had done the robbery for him, Worth grew attached to the painting and, remarkably, took it with him everywhere he moved, including to Cape Town in South Africa.

It was there that he pulled off a diamond heist worth US$500,000, $16 million in today's cash. He set up a jewellery store and gradually sold all the jewels, except perhaps one, which he gave to Louise Margaret Boljahn, who he married, still as Henry Raymond, in the 1880s. They had a daughter, Beatrice. It is believed his wife had no idea about his double life.

A robbery far beneath his normal methods finally led to his capture. In Belgium, he improvised the robbery of a money delivery cart in Liège with two untried associates. He was captured on the spot. Investigations soon revealed Henry Raymond was Adam Worth, and decades of suspicions which had never been proved came together. Former associates lined up to give evidence.

Worth's trial took place on 20 March 1893. He was sentenced to seven years for robbery and sent to Leuven Central Prison in Belgium. While in prison, he found out that the man he had tasked with looking after his wife had seduced and abandoned her, and she had suffered a complete breakdown and been committed to an asylum. Their daughter, Beatrice, had disappeared. It is important to remember that even the crimes of the most charming of men have evil consequences.

Released in 1897 for good behaviour, Worth approached William Pinkerton of the Pinkerton Detective Agency, which had tracked him for years, and dictated his memoir to him. He also arranged through Pinkerton to return the Gainsborough painting.

Adam Worth died on 8 January 1902. By then he was already living a second fictional life as James Moriarty, the arch nemesis of Sherlock Holmes described by Arthur Conan Doyle with the phrase that stuck to Worth – the Napoleon of Crime.

KLAAS BRUINSMA

They called him "De Dominee", meaning "The Pastor", partly because he wore black, partly because of his habit of delivering long sermons to those around him. He was, during the 1980s, the biggest drug lord in European history, and he possibly still holds the record. His name was Klaas Bruinsma and for a long time he struck fear into anyone who crossed his path.

He was tall – his second nickname was "De Lange" meaning "The Tall One" – with boyish good looks and a huge degree of charm, which he used to dupe people into believing he was an honest man. But if someone got on his wrong side, he had no qualms about making sure they didn't ever do so again. And killing them was the best guarantee the same mistake wouldn't be made twice.

He had been born into a wealthy family in Amsterdam, the Netherlands, in 1953. His father was an entrepreneur, and in a sense, Bruinsma would follow in his father's footsteps. His mother was British, and when the couple divorced when young Klaas was seven, she returned home. The boy and his three siblings were brought up by their father's housekeeper from then on.

It was sometime after he started high school that he first encountered the drug that was to define his life – hashish. By 16, he was using it regularly, and he was arrested for possession for the first time in 1970. He received a warning, but it didn't take. Graduating from school, instead of going to college like his friends, he hooked up with the daughter of a heroin smuggler from Singapore, Thea Moear (at 19, she had won Amsterdam's "Miss Hot Pants" in a beauty pageant), and the charming and attractive pair went into business – he ran logistics, and she kept control of the finances.

Moear was married at the time to Hugo Ferrol, another dealer. When Ferrol and Moear divorced in 1977, Bruinsma attempted to have him assassinated. He survived, but Bruinsma's gunman was killed in the shootout. The Dutch drug scene had just turned violent, and a second attempt was made in 1982. Astonishingly, Ferrol survived again.

Others who crossed Bruinsma's path were not so lucky. After a brief spell in prison, he hired a former kickboxer, André Brilleman, as his head of security and personal bodyguard. His other bodyguard was Etienne Urka. Both were known for their extreme violence in dealing with any threats or competitors.

Bruinsma's operation was by now becoming bigger and bigger, with divisions in Germany, France, Belgium and Scandinavia. He and Moear branched out into "associated industries" – brothels, casinos, hotels and gambling. They had also grown their trade in killing anyone who didn't play by their rules – as the firm's finance officer, Moear would pay people hired by Bruinsma to eliminate enemies or former associates.

Bruinsma had a spell in prison from 1979 to 1982 for organizing a large shipment of hash from Pakistan. During his time inside, several of his former employees attempted to take over parts of the business. Bruinsma dealt with the problem on his release – he had them shot; he even shot some of them himself. When he later served another three years, from 1984 to 1987, no one made the same mistake.

By now Moear had "retired" from the business (although as late as 2000 she was arrested in Panama for dealing and served five years in prison). Etienne Urka took her place. He told Bruinsma that he suspected André Brilleman was stealing cash from the business. Shortly after, Brilleman's body was discovered in the River Waal, encased in concrete.

By the 1990s, Bruinsma was trading around half a million US dollars per day, making him the biggest drug dealer in European history. It seemed enough, and Bruinsma decided he might retire and devote more time to his favourite hobby, sailing. But in classic Hollywood style, he wanted to do one more major trade. Codenamed "The Big Mountain", it involved smuggling US$200 million of hashish, again from Pakistan. But the drugs were seized by Dutch authorities, and Bruinsma's retirement was put on hold.

Despite the setback, Bruinsma – who was not arrested – continued to rake in the money. He turned to harder drugs, both personally and in his business. He was using a lot of cocaine, and it is said his disciplined manner started to disappear. He also began making the long monologues that earned him the nickname The Pastor and got into arguments over little things. One such argument seems to have cost him his life.

At 4 a.m. on the night of 27 June 1991, outside the Amsterdam Hilton, Bruinsma became involved in a verbal argument with

Martin Hoogland, a former police officer who was now working for a criminal organization. No one knows what the argument was about, but we do know that Hoogland drew his gun and shot Bruinsma dead. The Tall One had finally fallen from his great height. Hoogland was arrested and jailed for 20 years. While out on parole in 2004, he was riding his bike when he was shot dead in a hail of bullets.

No killer has ever been found, but it was the final proof that if you cross Klaas Bruinsma, he will make you pay, even from the grave.

FINAL WORD

And so it ends. Bombs, guns, drugs, knives, evil done with the point of a sword or the nib of a pen. There are Genghis Khans and Ivan the Terribles, Adolf Hitlers and Joseph Stalins, Jeffrey Dahmers and Martin Bryants, Charles Mansons and Steven Taris, Osama bin Ladens and Lucky Lucianos populating our history, and no doubt our futures. The battle against evil is constant, whether in ourselves or in the world at large.

And for every man named here, there are thousands of others committing lesser evils, or committing evils just as bad but escaping justice. Of course, there are perfect crimes, said the film director Alfred Hitchcock. The fact that we have never heard of them is what makes them perfect.

But there is also good. Many of those featured faced justice, either at their own hands, at the hands of others or by the power of the community. Seldom does an evil man survive and prosper. The perfect world where evil does not exist can never be, but the world where there is only evil is even more remote.

We are still learning what it is that leads men to evil; perhaps it will never be truly understood. But every story of evil teaches us how to prevent it, and if more and more of us choose compassion and good, then fewer and fewer of us will take up the weapons of hate. In particular, the bloody twentieth century, with its mass murders, mass suicides and the rise of the serial killer, may become as distant to us as the world of medieval torture.

And the only bogeymen we will have to fear are those in children's stories.

SERIAL KILLERS

Shocking True Stories
of the World's Most
Barbaric Murderers

JAMIE KING

SERIAL KILLERS
Shocking True Stories of the World's Most Barbaric Murderers

Jamie King

Paperback
ISBN: 978-1-83799-122-8

Who was the Zodiac Killer?
What drove Jeffrey Dahmer to dismember his 17 victims?
How did Ted Bundy get away with his horrific crimes?

Maybe it's because our animal instincts draw us to dangerous situations; maybe it's because reading about predators allows us to learn about their behaviours in a safe setting. Whatever the reason, serial killers and their crimes have fascinated us for centuries.

This true crime compendium not only relates the disturbing events that transpired but also delves into the psychology of the perpetrators. The stories within are shocking and often difficult to comprehend, but with this deep dive into the world of the macabre, readers may gain a greater understanding of the motivations and thought processes of these murderers.

This book is a must-read for anyone interested in the psychology of crime and the human mind.

TRUE CRIME STORIES

Shocking Tales of Real-Life Murderers, Thieves, Con Artists and Gangsters

JAMIE KING

TRUE CRIME STORIES

Shocking Tales of Real-Life Murderers, Thieves, Con Artists and Gangsters

Jamie King

Paperback
ISBN: 978-1-83799-007-8

Did you hear about London's Victorian, all-female gang?
What about the Great Canadian Maple Syrup Heist?
Do you know the story of the killer nun?

Prepare yourself for the urge to sleep with the light on, because these stories are not for the faint-hearted. With stories of criminal activity that span across the world, this book will take you on a journey to the darkest reaches of human nature, including:

- The true events that inspired the horror film *Friday the 13th*
- The people behind the cyber attack that cost over £90 million in damages
- The Roman poisoner who became the world's first known serial killer
- The carpenter who was executed by electrocution for kidnapping and murder

Whether you're a true crime junkie or just morbidly curious, let these stories of charismatic criminals and their sinister deeds ensnare your interest and send a shiver down your spine.

Have you enjoyed this book?
If so, why not write a review on your favourite website?

If you're interested in finding out more about our
books, find us on Facebook at **Summersdale Publishers,**
on Twitter/X at **@Summersdale** and on Instagram and
TikTok at **@summersdalebooks** and get in touch.
We'd love to hear from you!

Thanks very much for buying this Summersdale book.

www.summersdale.com